STARTUP
GUIDE

#startupeverywhere

Startup Guide Paris

Editor in Chief: **Jenna van Uden**
Deputy Editor: **Josh Raisher**
Writers: **Carrie Chappell and Paul Sullivan**
Photographer: **Rachel Moyer**
Researcher: **Eglė Duleckytė**
Proofreader: **Ted Hermann**
Production Manager: **Tim Rhodes**

Art direction, design & layout by
Design Studio Maurice Redmond - Berlin
www.dsmr.berlin

Illustrations by **sanjini.com**

Additional photography by
Celia Topping, **Camilo Gutierrez**,
and **unsplash.com**

Printed in Berlin, Germany by
Medialis-Offsetdruck GmbH
Heidelberger Str. 65, 12435 Berlin

Published by **Startup Everywhere**
Vestergade 82, 3 TV. Aarhus, Denmark
info@startupeverywhere.com

Visit: **startupeverywhere.com**

ISBN 978-87-40454-75-8

STARTUP GUIDE PARIS

STARTUP GUIDE PARIS

In partnership with **NUMA**

Sissel Hansen
/ Startup Everywhere

Less than five years ago, if someone had asked what Paris meant to me I would have said amazing cuisine, a fashion mecca, a romantic language. Today, mostly through what I've learned from my job, I know it's much more than that: Paris has a vibrant new ecosystem, and is home to many successful companies.

It has influential entrepreneurs like Xavier Niel, J.A Granjon and Marc Simmoncini, who are motivated and invested in Paris and are feeding a new generation of startups like Blablacar, Sigfox, Criteo and many more. And you're slowly starting to see the third wave of talent, including talent.io and Doctolib. At the same time, investment has tripled over the past few years, going from 750 million euro in 2014 to almost 3 billion euro in 2016. And the party's just getting started!

In April 2016, Emmanuel Macron (then the minister for economy and now France's new president) and Axelle Lemaire (minister of state for digital affairs) launched French Tech Hub in London, which offers the best talent, resources and services for French entrepreneurs around the world. Meanwhile, the French government initiative La French Tech offers French Tech Tickets to seventy startups every year, startup visas with a twelve-month program that offers end-to-end support for early-stage startups on the road to becoming successful businesses. Last but not least, 2017 is going to be the year when the world's biggest startup campus, Station F, will open, with more than 34,000 m^2 and space for more than 3,000 startups.

There's no doubt about it: Paris is one of the leading cities in the European startup ecosystem. When we started working on the Startup Guide Paris, language was one issue that came up: in the startup world, where companies are born global from day one, English tends to be the most commonly spoken language. Even though the French are known for their pride in their language, we decided to print this book in English to support the constant growth of the ecosystem – not only the French talent, but also those wishing to begin their entrepreneurial journey in France.

CEO and founder

Anne Hidalgo
/ Mayor of Paris

In just a few years, the Paris innovation ecosystem has blossomed. Driven by a strong political will and a new generation of entrepreneurs, investors, researchers and designers, it is now growing more strongly than ever.

With over sixty incubators and accelerators – and fifteen more in the making – hundreds of innovative coworking spaces, some thirty digital manufacturing workshops and more and more success stories, Paris is home to an exceptional dynamism. And it hasn't gone unnoticed: as the world's leading city for intellectual capital and innovation, Paris recently ranked first in Europe for the vitality of its innovation market in terms of the number of tech deals and transactions completed.

Paris also aims to become the "maker" capital and to assert itself as a welcoming home base for all growing sectors. We think of the city itself as a real open-air laboratory, a space for experimenting with new solutions, for all innovators, from startups to established companies. This strategy has convinced private investors to increase their investment in the city – reflected in the incredible Station F project, which will be the world's largest incubator when it opens in June 2017.

And we aren't done yet. We want to go even further and open our incubators to talent and ideas from all over the world. This is part of an exciting strategy to help Paris become a global startup "factory", a breeding ground for the answers to tomorrow's challenges. It is through innovation that we will be able to meet the major challenges of the twenty-first century, whether ecological, economic, social or democratic.

We are going through a major shift, fostering innovation and openness. It is no longer a question of merely undergoing these transformations, but of anticipating and guiding them. It is also an opportunity to reinvent ourselves by imagining new ways of working, producing, consuming and travelling. Today, I want to assure the world's innovators that Paris will always be a venue for all forms of energy, dreams and daring.

Anne Hidalgo

French Tech Ecosystem

- Of the **9,400** French startups, **35 percent** are based in the Paris Region.

- **Sixty-eight percent** of investment (in terms of total value) in French startups in 2015 happened in the Paris Region.

- The number of startups created in France increased by **30 percent** per year from 2012 to 2015.

- From 2014 to 2015, total funds raised by French startups increased by **102 percent** (from **€0.9 billion** to **€1.8 billion**), while UK and German startup fundraising increased by **71 percent** (from **€2.7 billion** to **€4.6 billion**) and **19 percent** (from **€2.3 billion** to **€2.8 billion**) respectively.

- From 2015 to 2016, French startup fundraising increased by **22 percent** (from **€1.8 billion** to **€2.2 billion**), while UK and German startup fundraising decreased by **14 percent** (from **€4.6 billion** to **€4.0 billion**) and **21 percent** (from **€2.8 billion** to **€2.2 billion**) respectively.

- According to tech.eu, Paris has "dethroned" Berlin and London in terms of the number of startup investments, with **590** deals in France in 2016 versus **520** in the UK and **384** in Germany.

- Forty-one percent of French startups that participated in the EY Advisory study "Enquête en ligne, mars 2017" have international (non-French) employees. Of those startups employing internationals, **58 percent** have at least three international employees. Forty-nine percent of respondents identified as "serial entrepreneurs."

- France was the second-best-represented international country at Eureka Park at CES 2017 with **178** startups present. France was also the second-best-represented international delegation at Eureka Park in 2016.

- Mindsets regarding entrepreneurship are changing in France: in 2017, **60 percent** of young people (**18–24 year olds**) want to create their own company or take over an existing company (compared to **55 percent** in 2016 and **50 percent** in 2015).

[Capital:] **Total Funds Raised by French Startups by Year:**
2013 – €1 billion / 2014 – €0.9 billion / 2015 – €1.8 billion / 2016 – €2.2 billion

[Stock Exchange:] **French Startups (Scaleups) Listed on NASDAQ**
Criteo, DBV, Talend, Cellectis

[R&D:] **International Companies are Choosing Paris as their Research and Development Centers**

- Facebook opened its first artificial intelligence research center outside the US in 2015 in Paris (after hiring French citizen Yann LeCun as head of AI Research in 2013).
- Rakuten chose Paris for its first European R&D center in 2014.
- Google opened a research center in Paris in 2010.
- Microsoft chose Paris as an R&D center in 2008.

Sources: tech.com; EY Advisory studies "Observatoire des startups françaises, avril 2017," "Enquête en ligne, mars 2017" and "Baromètre du capital risque en France bilan annuel 2016" – ey.com; OpinionWay study "Les jeunes et le travail, janvier 2017."

Paris, France

Greater Paris population: **6,797,865**

Surface area of greater Paris: **762 km²**

Number of tourists: **46,700,000**

Trade shows: **407**

Museums: **206**

Historical monuments: **2185**

Theatres: **265**

Opera houses: **3**

Movie theatres: **720**

Source: Paris Tourist Office Key Statistics 2015

STARTUP GUIDE PARIS

Paris Essentials

Paris's role as an artistic and cultural capital for Europe and the world is undeniable. Boasting over 200 museums, 1,000 art galleries, 2,100 historic monuments and 420 parks, the City of Lights is rich with opportunities for entertainment. Yet while the city may seem rooted in Napoleonic luxury, Paris is hardly old-fashioned, and far from frivolous.

In fact, innovation and Paris have always gone together. Whether opening its laboratory doors to the likes of Marie Curie and Louis Pasteur or its catwalks to Coco Chanel and Kenzo, Paris has been a home to some of the world's most daring pioneers. While the city does hold on to its history, the locals like to mix it up, and are masters at integrating old with new. Parisians define their districts not only by their boulangerie but also by their local craft beer stores and food co-ops. Business in Paris is stimulated by this adaptability, all while being fed by a growing and diverse community of artistic, social and tech entrepreneurs. Whether you are drawn to the historic and academic atmospheres of the Latin Quarter, the bohemian delights of Montmartre and La Villette, the unique gallery-lined streets of the Marais, the bridges and boulevards that meet the Seine, or the lively corner cafes of Montparnasse, Paris is full of grand squares and cozy nooks to explore, and its residents are as happy to flirt with the past as they are to relish the present.

Before You Come

First, a move to Paris is a move to France. It would behoove you to build on your *"bonjour"* and become at least a beginner speaker of French. While Parisians, from baristas to bankers, are increasingly skilled in English, allotting some time to understanding your new environment and new relationship with bureaucracy will be highly beneficial.

If you're moving to Paris as a citizen of the EU, you have the legal right to work in France, but you should notify the local mayor's office, La Mairie, of your new residency within three months of your arrival to avoid problems or fines. For citizens of other countries, you must acquire a visa, which is not, typically, a short process. In order to obtain legal working status in the country, you must have a company willing to sponsor you and offer you either a contract CDI (long-term work engagement) or CDD (short-term arrangement). If you're arriving just to check out the scene, then you are free to explore the city and country for up to ninety days.

Cost of Living

While Paris may be known as a luxurious cultural capital, an affordable way of life is not out of reach. The chief costs of living in the city are housing, food and transport, yet defining some lifestyle choices early on could save your Paris budget and make for better stories.

Finding living spaces away from the city center could cut your rent by hundreds of euros and save you stress. Even though the French invented gourmet dining, not every meal must end with champagne. Many locals enjoy shopping at their local co-ops or at the famous open-air markets where items are seriously fresh and less expensive. Plus, if your French is good enough, you can bargain with the vendors.

Public transportation is the name of the game in this city. Almost all Parisians refer to the city by metro stop. Buses, shared biking, car and scooter systems are alive and rolling.

Cultural Differences

Do not be afraid to walk into business or social situations announcing your arrival with a *"bonjour."* While some foreigners assume this salutation is a thing of the past or a child's lesson from a Disney movie, *"Bonjour Madame"* or *"Bonjour Monsieur"* is a nod of appreciation and invites better exchanges.

One myth that has a grain of truth is that Parisians are always complaining. While it can be difficult to decipher, this critical attitude does not, in fact, mean that the French are unhappy with you or their situation. But the French are quite analytical, so don't be surprised if they find a reason to oppose certain ideas. This approach is imbedded in them from their early education, and can be a sign of respect that you have presented them with an interesting challenge, one that warrants scrutiny from all sides.

Renting an Apartment

The apartment hunt can be long and tedious due to Paris's compact size and interminable popularity. Keep in mind that you are most likely competing with millions of people who could share a similar profile to you. When arranging meetings with either individuals or agents, come with a complete dossier, including bank statements, your work contract, your CV, your passport and visa, and translated documents that prove you are an invested and responsible potential renter.

In addition, be sure to consider exactly what lifestyle you would like in the city. Each district has a particular feeling and a particular price bracket. What's more, it's best to consider what could be your potential morning and evening commutes, and which metro and bus lines are most convenient. After that, when visiting apartments, take special note of where everyday needs – grocery stores, pharmacies, cafes – might be found, for even if the price is right, extra trips to far-off places for necessities will become expensive and tiresome.

One-bedroom apartments range in size, from the miniature but scenic charm of a 15 m^2 "chambre de bonne," a converted maid's quarters, to a truer one-bedroom apartment that can be anywhere from 20 m^2–100 m^2. Many young people opt for colocations, using sites such as **appartager.com**, **colocation.fr** and **recherche-colocation.com**. With this option, you usually double your square meters, and quite possibly your view.

See **Flats and Rentals** page 210

Finding a Coworking Space

As diverse as Paris is in neighborhoods, so too in coworking spaces. Inevitably, many of them, though not all, are located in the heart of the city and feature diverse atmospheres and membership options. Whether you are seeking networking opportunities or the privacy of more intimate corners, Paris is ripe with resources. Several options are listed later on, introducing you to the nomadic and multidimensional experiences of Kwerk, the tucked-away hideout dreamed up by Nuage Café and the developing epicenter of Paris startup culture at Station F.

See **Spaces** page 70

Insurance

All residents of France are required to be enrolled in the national social security system, commonly referred to as *La Sécu*. As a foreigner with a work contract, you must follow a registration process with your company to enter the system. Following your acceptance, your participation and payment into the statement will be automatically deducted from your monthly salary. Self-employed workers fall into a different category and must, by virtue of registering as an auto-entrepreneur, work with *Régime Social des Indépendants* (RSI). For the time being, residents are expected to pay upfront for their medical visits and prescriptions, but will be reimbursed, typically for around 70 percent of the costs, within a few weeks. If you are only staying temporarily, it would be best to seek an agreement with a private, international provider.

If you plan on bringing or buying a vehicle, you must enroll in *assurance automobile*. The same goes for home or apartment owners; you must enlist in *assurance habitation*. For those seeking bigger projects, know that it is mandatory to insure major construction works that take place on your property. If you are starting your own business, it would be wise, too, to seek out for professional indemnity. Once settled, seek consultation for insurances required for civil liberty and for schoolchildren.

See **Insurance Companies** page 210

Visas and Work Permits

The Paris job market is competitive, slightly slow-moving and a bit idiosyncratic, so research your best options as much as possible before you come to make the most of your time and budget. The French workplace is composed of two different types of contracts, and you need to know if you're being offered a CDI or a CDD.

If you are moving to Paris from one of the countries that comprise the EU/EEA or if you're coming from Switzerland, you can live and work freely in France. Those arriving in France from other counties will need permission to work in the country. This permission is granted once your employer submits a complete dossier to the French Ministry of Labor and this office approves of the need you satisfy in the French workplace. Temporary work permits exist for those wishing to stay in the country for only 90 days. Skills, talents and arts visas are also options if you can present a strong CV of accomplishments and promising arguments for extraordinary contribution to the French marketplace.

See **Important Government Offices** page 210

Starting a Company

The entrepreneurial path in France is no walk in the park, and, from the point of view of the government it's for good reason. If you wish to build a business in France, you need to be prepared to answer to both the structural and financial feasibility and longevity of your company in the country. Many pit stops are required, but it's all in a bureaucratic effort to promote success. And in this, though perhaps strangely, there is a kind of security and invitation.

Because the process can be tricky, many suggest hiring an expert guide, someone who is familiar with French business law, to help you navigate all of the steps. Structurally, you will need to make and document some early decisions: What industry does your company belong to? To which business structure and tax model does your business subscribe? This plan will eventually be reviewed by a banker to deem if your business is worthy of a business bank account. Every business must register its name with the *Centre de Formalités des Entreprises* (CFE), and each company must establish its business structure by submitting for review their bylaws.

See **Programs** page 54

Opening a Bank Account

If you are planning to stay a long time in Paris, you will benefit from opening a local account. Most banks will require proof of address, or what is called a *justificatif de domicile*, which could be a bill addressed to you in the last three months or an original copy of your renter's insurance. As France is a country of bureaucracy and paperwork, it would be wise to bring with you copies of all documents you've prepared for your visa appointments. Translated copies of your birth certificate and what is called an *apostille* are good to have on hand, as well as a copy of your work contract. Popular banks in Paris are Société Générale, BNP Parisbas, CIC, Banque Populaire, LCL, La Banque Postale and Crédit Agricole.

See **Banks** page 209

Taxes

While living in France allows you to benefit fully from one of Europe's greatest social security systems, residency does come with some high social charges. Filing your tax return (*déclaration de revenus*) is relatively simple after a few years in the country. However, as a first-time filer, you might be better off making a visit to your local tax office (*centre des impôts*) to make sure you understand the process for the future. Then, once you are in the system, you will automatically be sent a completed form stating your earnings. The French tax system works in brackets, and thus charges people who earn more at a higher percentage. If you hold the tax status of auto-entrepreneur, you are expected to submit quarterly reports of revenues to URSAF, the social security contributions agency.

See **Accountants** page 209

Telephone Contracts

Free, Orange, SFR and Bouygues Telecom are some of the most popular mobile/internet service providers in France. Due to their popularity, these companies ensure the best coverage in the country. While prepaid cell phone options exist, if you are settling in for the long term, you will want to engage in a more permanent arrangement. As is the case in most countries, these companies will require a contract that lasts anywhere from twelve to twenty-four months, and they will request your bank information to ensure monthly withdrawals for service payments.

Getting Around

One quintessential image of Paris is the metro, and to this day, the city remains measured in its stops. Daily and weekly subway and bus tickets are available and useful for a tourist's agenda, but purchasing a monthly Navigo Pass is preferable for a fluid, day-to-day routine in the city as it allows you access to both the metro and bus lines. However, if the city streets call to you, there's no need to go underground. Several Parisian initiatives have made promises to offer shared car, scooter and bike services. Autolib, Cityscoot and Vélib offer very inexpensive and flexible subscriptions, so you can easily dash around the city while also enjoying the scenery.

Learning the Language

The old-fashioned idea that Parisians do not respect or like English speakers is a stereotype that many would like to see disappear. A lot of locals are bi- or tri-lingual and are happy to exchange with those not native to France. Still, moving to France will require a certain familiarity with the language, and if you wish to stay for a long time, learning French is essential to integration into the metropolitan and national culture. While French is indeed a challenging language, it is also one that provides you with a vast array of cultural, artistic, business and personal expressions. One of the most affordable options is with Alliance Française, a French language school that is connected to Paris City Hall. Centrally located and diversely programmed, this school provides lessons at a variety of hours in hopes of meeting the needs of its cosmopolitan community. Other schools worth checking out are France Langue, Berlitz and L'Atelier 9.

See **Language Schools** page 211

Meeting People

Making true connections in a city as bustling and diverse as Paris can be an interesting challenge. Even the locals admit that friendships are hard to build, as everyone seems to be chasing a specific and individual destiny. At the same time, coworking spaces, tech and hobby collectives, Meetup communities and Facebook groups bring together many of the cities locals and expats, and present consistent and engaging ways to interact and network. Liberté Living-Lab openly invites innovators in the city to join them in conferences and seminars around civic-tech conversations. As you might imagine, though, one of the best ways to meet people is to join organizations and groups that convene around your interests. These spaces are where you'll meet the like-minded individuals you've been looking for.

See **Startup Events** page 211

LEMONADE

5

[Name] # Archive Valley

[Elevator Pitch] *"Archive Valley is the first platform that helps content makers and production companies find unique footage across the world. Our innovative solution directly connects footage requests with worldwide archive providers, simplifying the process of sourcing and licensing exceptional content."*

[The Story] In 2010, after completing her master's degree on the topic of "Archives in the Digital Age" at the Royal College of Art in London, Melanie Rozencwajg cofounded the first digital design studio exclusively dedicated to archives and innovation with Jhava Chikli. ARTCHIVIUMlab designed thirty interactive digital installations for Veuve Clicquot, Zenith, Aviva and Harcourt studio, as well as for museums in Paris, London, New York and Tel Aviv. In 2015 the cofounders integrated into the startup incubator NUMA. Pioneering a digital platform that would connect content creators with unique footage providers all over the world, Melanie and Jhava launched Archive Valley in January 2016.

It all started when Jhava and Melanie found themselves working for a project where they had to search for footage all over the world, from Russia, Cuba, Italy, Canada, Egypt and more. "We realized the huge challenge content creators face each time they need to search for and buy original footage for their productions," says Melanie. "Archive Valley was born with a strong desire to fix that problem, to offer content creators a simple and fast solution to find unique footage scattered all over the world. We knew there had to be a way to use our background and experience to connect content creators with the proper archive providers and right holders."

[Funding History]

Seed Funding   Angel Investment

[Milestones]
- Debuting the first international community of archive researchers
- Integrating into the startup incubator NUMA
- Birth of Archive Valley in January 2016
- Developing our MSP in May 2016

[Links] Web: archivevalley.com Facebook: ArchiveValley Twitter: @ArchiveValley Instagram: archivevalley

[Name] # Baby Sittor

[Elevator Pitch]
"Baby Sittor is a mobile application that connects busy parents with trusted babysitters. Our network of over 100,000 trusted parents and sitters facilitates community and promotes stress-free planning for everyone."

[The Story]
When cofounder Pauline de Montesson arrived in Paris four years ago, she wanted to be a babysitter. In fact, Pauline and all of her friends were looking for childcare opportunities. The high cost of living in Paris was calling, and they wanted to share their energy with the city's most enigmatic residents – the young. To organize herself and the needs of her friends, Pauline launched a Facebook group. Within a week, the group had accepted ten more members, and by the end of the second week, it had grown to 300.

"The idea was that the group would make life easier for both sides of the equation. Parents would post an ad, and interested sitters would respond," explains Thomas Clamagirand, CEO and cofounder. Pauline knew the community would only last if parents and sitters could trust each other, so she began screening requests for membership. "In fact, she created a kind of application. Each babysitter and parent would need a sponsorship," states Thomas. Confidence is what separated the community from similar groups and led to its expansion in Nantes, Bordeaux and other cities in the country. Baby Sittor launched in February 2016, and in April 2017 released the second version of its app. "Our new version really reinforces this trust. It's more or less like a LinkedIn for babysitting," states Thomas.

[Funding History]

Seed Funding   Angel Investment

[Milestones]
- Creating the original Facebook group in 2013
- Launching the V-1 app in 2016
- Raising €500,000 with Julien Codorniou, Guillaume Princen and Thibaut Elziere in 2016
- Constructing a new technical team and launching the second version of the app in 2017

[Links]   Web: **babysittor.com** Facebook: **bbsittor** Twitter: **@Baby_sittor** Instagram: **baby_sittor**

IF A USER IS
HAVING A PROBLEM
IT'S OUR PROBLEM

Trouvez des babysitters de confiance

Sélectionnez votre babysitter en Or

Accédez aux annonces proches de chez vous

[Name] # Belty

[Elevator Pitch] *"Belty is the first ever smart belt: a high-end lifestyle accessory that merges wellbeing, fashion and technology. Nine out of ten men wear belts every single day. We think it's obvious that being smart can mean being smartly dressed."*

[The Story] For Emiota, the creator of Belty, the line between fashion and technology has always been blurred – but CEO and business developer Carine Coulm thinks this line completely disappears in the design of a piece of high-end, sustainable technology that helps you consolidate your life and tune into your body. "I've always been concerned with health. When I was young, I struggled with my weight. That's why when I became an entrepreneur and saw the potential, I thought, I want to develop a chic but covert way to live with well-being technologies, what we ended up calling an 'awearable tech'," says Carine. Now the first smartbelt, the Belty Power, is on the market, a tech-wearable that allows you to carry on normally with your day while you charge your phone. Cobranded with L'Aiglon, Belty Power weds fashion with function in this handcrafted accessory.

In the coming months, Belty will release its first prototype, Belty Good Vibes, a belt that integrates artificial intelligence directly into a wearable. By reading the body's activity, Belty Good Vibes will help wearers optimize well-being by sending vibrations that help them teach themselves to adjust behaviors. "We are really interested in creating new habits and living better by incorporating the use of different frequencies in communication with our bodies. It's a new language – haptic," explains Carine.

[Funding History]

Bootstrap   Angel Investment

[Milestones]
- Signing cobranding agreement with L'Aiglon
- Winning Best of CES Award with a prototype that adapts to your waistline
- Revising Belty after CES win
- Creating an advisory board

[Links]   Web: **wearbelty.com** Facebook: **Belty.Paris** Twitter: **@Belty** Instagram: **belty.paris**

[Name]
Compte-Nickel

[Elevator Pitch]
"Compte-Nickel is the first bank-free account. Now, with Compte-Nickel everyone can have a simple account with which you can pay and get paid. We issue Mastercards and IBANs in five minutes in 3,000 affiliated tobacco stores in France."

[The Story]
Compte-Nickel revolutionized banking in 2011 when Ryad Boulanouar, an engineer working on payment technology, realized that three to six million French citizens were excluded from the banking system. "Ryad began to notice that many people could not be paid or use their own money as they pleased and were forced to use expensive prepaid cards. On top of that, once these same people finally got access to a bank, they usually became victims of the system and were subjected to the vicious cycle of overdraft fees and other charges," says Adrien Le Roy, marketing manager.

The transformative idea was to sign a partnership with the Confédération des Buralistes de France and make accounts available in a practical, convenient location – the tobacco stores – where people frequently passed. This exclusive agreement between the Confédération and Compte-Nickel is now a network of 3,000+ tobacco stores in France that offer easy, transparent access to a bank account. "For twenty euros a year, anyone can open a Compte-Nickel in five minutes and get real-time access to their own funds and modern payment methods with maximum simplicity and efficiency," explains Adrien. Supporting 600,000 customers country-wide and opening more than 1,000 accounts per day, more than any other bank in France, Compte-Nickel stays true to its mission: Be useful, be transparent, be simple and be universal.

[Funding History]

Seed Funding   Angel Investment   Venture Capital

[Milestones]
- Obtaining a payment institution license in June 2013
- Establishing our exclusive partnership with the Confédération des Buralistes de France in 2013, bringing Compte-Nickel directly into tobacco stores
- Grand public opening in February 2014
- Reaching 500,000 accounts in 2,500 tobacco stores in February 2017

[Links]   Web: **compte-nickel.fr** Facebook: **CompteNickel** Twitter: **@CompteNickel**

[Name] # Dataiku

[Elevator Pitch] *"Founded in 2013, we develop collaborative data science software, bringing together teams of data scientists, data analysts, engineers and non-coders to prototype and deliver data projects more efficiently."*

[The Story] Dataiku, a portmanteau of the words "data" and "haiku," seeks to make every stage of data science project design and production more efficient and more satisfying. "Our four cofounders had all played different roles related to data in major software companies and had begun to notice the huge disconnect in skillsets and communication between data scientists, analysts and data architects. They were working in silo departments and not collaborating, and it led to many data projects bringing little value to their companies," says Alivia Smith in user marketing.

To ease this friction, the cofounders developed software that allows them to work on predictive analytics collaboratively, applying individual skills and tools that are structured around an automated flow view. Dataiku makes the data application development process more agile and effective. "The most satisfying thing is meeting our clients, all from extremely different backgrounds, and seeing how our product is helping them gain new skills and work together to implement projects that bring value to their companies. I love seeing data scientists working alongside analysts and engineers and really building business value out of Big Data," explains Alivia. To maintain its own community, Dataiku stays small and intimate even while growing steadily. With a total of eighty-five employees worldwide, Dataiku calls Paris, New York and London home.

[Funding History]

Bootstrap   Seed Funding   Venture Capital

[Milestones]
- Launching our first version in February 2014
- Raising 3.6 million euros in seed funding in January 2015 with twenty employees and thirty clients
- Launching the second version of our software and the opening of our New York office in April 2015
- Growing 200 percent annually in early 2016, establishing Bay Area and London offices

[Links]   Web: **dataiku.com** Facebook: **dataiku** Twitter: **@dataiku** Instagram: **dataiku**

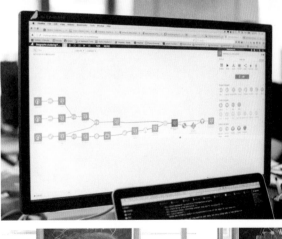

[Name] # drust

[Elevator Pitch] *"We make superdrivers. drust is a platform that connects the heart of the car to the driver and to the rest of the automotive ecosystem, which gives users direct access to information that empowers their driving experience and car care."*

[The Story] After nearly seven years as powertrain engineers with PSA, Europe's second largest car manufacturer, drust cofounders Michaël Fernandez, Florent Pignal and Pascal Galacteros hit on the answer to a problem: they realized the key to improving car maintenance and making cars more environmentally friendly actually lay in the hands of the driver. "Our company was just too big to bother with this idea. Plus, we didn't know who in the company would even be interested, so it became very clear that we had to go outside of the company," says CEO Michaël Fernandez. They developed an app that could make drivers better at driving.

Acting as another feature of the dashboard, the drust app provides drivers with added-value services. The "dongle" communicates with the app and gives the driver information that can help save up to 250 euros per year, while decreasing CO_2 emissions. "It allows you to have a simple interaction with your automobile, like you would with your own health via a fitness app. You can check-in from anywhere, see how you are improving, how you perform compared to drivers in your community," explains Michaël. With established partnerships with insurance and repair companies in Europe, drust enables a driver to easily schedule maintenance appointments and plug into a superdriver experience.

[Funding History]

Seed Funding   Angel Investment   Venture Capital

[Milestones]
- Being accepted into the NUMA Accelerator Program in September 2014
- Successfully launching our Indiegogo crowdfunding campaign in March 2015
- Strategic partnership with Macif Group, a French auto insurance leader, in Summer 2016
- Launching our product in November 2016

[Links] Web: drust.io Facebook: Drust.io Twitter: @drust_io Instagram: drust.io

drust

41

[Name] # Innerspace VR

[Elevator Pitch] *"Innerspace VR is a virtual reality entertainment studio. We tell interactive stories and help forge the future of entertainment with award-winning and commercially successful titles, proprietary technology and a world-class team of creators."*

[The Story] Born in Korea in early 2015 in the heart of the Samsung technology community, Innerspace VR is a virtual reality content studio based in Paris with an office in Los Angeles. The two founders, Balthazar Auxietre and Hayoun Kwon, both had curious and artistic minds, and built the studio together, initially as a collective. Hadrien Lanvin soon joined the team as CEO, and today Innerspace VR is one of the leading VR creation studios in Europe and around the world.

"For the moment, we speak a language few people understand. We are entering a landscape very few people know how to interpret, so even though we have developed our vision, much of our work is about making the first contact with the community, revealing what is VR, what is the potential of this industry," says Hadrien. From late 2015 to early 2016, Innerspace made the move to France, understanding the wealth of the talent pool in Paris. "When it comes to design and animation, Paris is almost unparalleled, so we benefit on a daily basis from both in-house and external talent. For a creative company, operating in France is probably one of the better options available," says Hadrien.

[Funding History]

Bootstrap   Seed Funding   Venture Capital

[Milestones]
- Innerspace VR is born in summer 2015
- Becoming more ambitious with investment from Japanese VR fund Colopl in May 2016
- Releasing the award-winning game Firebird: La Péri in August 2016
- Striking coproduction deals with major players such as Facebook in spring 2017

[Links] Web: **innerspacevr.com** Facebook: **InnerspaceVR** Twitter: **@InnerspaceVR**

[Name] # La Ruche qui dit Oui!

[Elevator Pitch] *"La Ruche is a web platform that connects people directly to farmers and fresh produce. Organized by local hosts and serving local communities, our 'food assemblies' are springing up all over Europe to increase sustainable consumption and fairer revenues."*

[The Story]
The three cofounders of la Ruche qui dit Oui! – Guilhem Chéron, Mounir Mahjoubi and Marc-David Choukroun – were inspired to use their skills to both encourage transparent food sourcing and increase the revenue earned by farmers. Now operating in nine European countries and supporting over 200,000 customers and 7,000 local producers through 1,400 Food Assemblies, la Ruche qui dit Oui! harnesses the power of technology to focus on community-based systems. "From the beginning, we knew we wanted to do something that was local, not centralized. We didn't want to build a Paris-centric company. We wanted to build a platform that actually stayed true to that," explains Marc-David Choukroun, the company's current CEO.

Signing up with la Ruche allows neighbors to find an Assembly close to their home, where they can go every week to pick up fresh produce and get to know their community, the host and the producers. Ultimately, la Ruche's business model allows farmers to increase and define their own revenue. "We really want to rethink and refresh the way we interact with agriculture and the way farmers interact with their customers. Our vision is big and this project will take years of hard work. If we get it right, the impact will positively change our food system." says Marc-David.

[Funding History]

Seed Funding   Angel Investment   Venture Capital

[Milestones]
- Launching the first Ruche in Le Fauga in September 2011
- Launching in Belgium in 2013 and subsequently in the UK, Spain and Germany in 2014
- Securing international VC investment led by Union Square, Felix Capital and Quadia in 2015
- Receiving B Corp label in 2016

[Links] Web: **laruchequiditoui.fr** Facebook: **laruchequiditoui** Twitter: **@ruchequiditoui**

[Name] # Never Eat Alone

[Elevator Pitch] *"Our mission is to connect employees inside large companies to help them be happier at work. Be it for coffee, lunch or an exercise session, Never Eat Alone wants to create connections and friendship within the big corporate walls."*

[The Story] When Marie Schneegans, founder and CEO of Never Eat Alone, first entered the workforce, she was an intern at a large Swiss bank. The day-to-day atmosphere was not as dreamy as she expected; in fact, it was downright boring. "I went entire days without any interaction with my colleagues. I was young, energetic, and I wanted to meet people. Yet, I felt very pent-up in this cold ambiance," explains Marie. So Marie began to do something perhaps a bit strange. At lunchtime each day, she began knocking on people's doors. "I would just say, would you like to have lunch with me? And it worked, even if people were surprised, they mostly said yes."

Marie's bold move launched a trend, and eventually, many of her colleagues began telling her they had wanted to do the same, but felt too shy. Realizing the novelty this represented at a large business, Marie set the wheels in motion. A year and a half ago, she launched Never Eat Alone, a web and mobile app that allows people within large corporations to connect on interests both professional and personal. Now Never Eat Alone is working internationally, within sixty big companies including L'Oréal, Allianz, Danone and Société Générale. "It's really making people's daily lives better. We are breaking the silence," says Marie.

[Funding History]

Bootstrap   Seed Funding

[Milestones]
- Finding our first customer, Vinci, one of the largest contracting companies in the world
- Building a tech team with the revenue from our first clients
- Raising our first seed round of 1.3 million euro in September 2016
- Opening a New York office in January 2017

[Links] Web: **nevereatalone.io** Facebook: **nevereataloneapp** Twitter: **@NeverEatAlone**

[Name]
Stanley Robotics

[Elevator Pitch]
"We are experts in industrial service robotics. Our mission is to revolutionize urban mobility and to better serve humanity through designing and implementing mobile robots in public environments."

[The Story]
Clément Boussard, Aurélien Cord and Stéphane Evanno had grown tired of waiting for self-driving car projects to come to market. After years in research labs and industry focusing on autonomous driving, these men were ready to take technology out of the car and put it into public life. But despite their similar backgrounds and geographic location, they had not formed a team yet. Luckily, believing in their dream brought them great coincidence: "Clément and Aurélien were working in the same research lab. We all ended up meeting through TheFamily. Oussama Ammar, the cofounder, connected Clément and Aurélien with myself. We immediately saw that we shared the same vision and hunger. They came with tech, and I came with industry and business knowledge," explains Stéphane Evanno, COO.

For the moment, Stanley Robotics has focused its model on one specific project that will help it develop for an entire market. With help from the company robot, Stanley, and a partnership with Paris Charles De Gaulle International Airport, these men are revolutionizing the parking experience. "We 'delete' the headache of parking. Our robot can store 50% more cars in any given area, and users do not have to waste time finding a spot or locating their car. They can just dispose of their car at the entrance of the car park, at a very convenient spot, and one of our robots will come and take the car," says Stéphane.

[Funding History]

Bootstrap   Seed Funding   Angel Investment   Venture Capital

[Milestones]
- Oussama introducing Clément and Aurélien
- Founding in January 2015
- Finding our key angel funders and first customer, Charles De Gaulle International Airport, in July 2015
- Starting service in February 2017

[Links] Web: **stanley-robotics.com** Facebook: **stanleyrobotics** Twitter: **@StanleyRobotics**

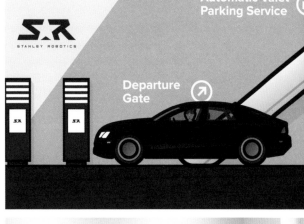

Automatic Valet Parking Service

Departure Gate

[Name] # talent.io

[Elevator Pitch] *"We are Europe's fastest growing selective recruitment marketplace in the technology industry. Serving Paris, Lyon, Berlin and London, we help connect Europe's top candidates to great futures in leading startup and technology companies."*

[The Story] talent.io was founded in March 2015 by Amit Aharoni, Jonathan Azoulay and Nicolas Meunier. After Amit and Nicolas, two Stanford graduates, sold their first startup (Cruisewise) to TripAdvisor, they were looking for their next project and a possible return home to France. While scaling their former startup in Silicon Valley, Amit and Nicolas found themselves in need of tech talent but unable to find the right candidates. The best minds were unavailable, unresponsive or not looking for a job at the moment. That's how Nicolas and Amit discovered a new problem, and a future business idea.

On the other side of the Atlantic Ocean, Jonathan had noticed that "selective marketplaces" were gaining traction across the world and that Europe was missing a major player. He then started working by himself on adapting a recruitment model for Europe. One day, as he was talking to a venture capital friend, he learned about two San Francisco entrepreneurs who were experimenting with a similar idea. After just one Skype conversation, the three men joined forces in establishing talent.io. Jonathan brought his knowledge about the recruitment industry, while Nicolas and Amit offered their experience building marketplaces. Two years later, talent.io has expanded to Lyon, Berlin and London, and helped more than 2,000 companies find their new team members.

[Funding History]

Seed Funding   Angel Investment   Venture Capital

[Milestones]
- Our transatlantic introduction and realizing our path
- Launching with 40+ French startups and establishing credibility
- Our seed-round (two million euros) and roadshow, which garnered the interest of three investors in one month
- Opening in Europe's major tech hubs in Berlin and London in 2016

[Links] Web: **talent.io** Facebook: **talent.ioEU** Twitter: **@talent_io** Instagram: **talent_io**

[Name] # Ulule

[Elevator Pitch] *"We are the leading crowdfunding website in France and Europe, providing an efficient web tool for project creators and advice and support from our team of expert coaches. We also work with businesses to leverage interests and refashion sponsoring."*

[The Story] Back in 2001 when Alexandre Boucherot started a website about culture, he wanted to ask viewers directly to finance the next features. This, he admits, was a big failure. For one thing, social networks did not yet exist, and internet users did not understand that a complete, free model was not feasible. Alexandre would have to wait a bit to realize his project; it was a vision for the future, for 2010, by which point web media would have undergone several revolutions.

However, since its launch in October 2010, Ulule, the answer to Alexandre's 2001 question, has financed more than 17,000 creative, innovative or community-minded projects for close to 80 million euro, and supported users from 201 countries. "In fact, we created two companies, Ulule and Botify. At the beginning we had to help ourselves exist, and we wanted to stay committed to our values, our customers. By 2013, we split the companies up, split up the four partners, and we recently raised capital for the first time in December 2015. In the beginning, it was really important not to be pushed by another person's strategy so that we could really become our vision," says Arnaud Burgot, president. Based in Paris, Montréal, Barcelona, Rome and Antwerp, Ulule's multilocal mission is to live close to and support creators and entrepreneurs.

[Funding History]

Bootstrap

Venture Capital

[Milestones]
- Creating Semio SAS and beginning to develop the ulule.com platform in January 2010
- Financing 100,000 users and 1,000 projects in July 2012
- Signing partnership with BNP Paribas, new design for ulule.com and 500,000 ululers
- Ulule-certified B Corp and SOS Mediterrannée collect 274 thousand euros to help refugees

[Links] Web: **ulule.com** Facebook: **ululeEn** Twitter: **@ulule** Instagram: **ulule**

- **Develop your proof of concept**
  Spend time on your idea. You have to give this step of the process the most attention. If not, you will fall into one of the common pitfalls. Focus on your concept and its usability and feasibility, as well as its attractiveness. Define the core of your business.

- **Contact people and be open**
  Openness brings openness. Engage in discussion, even if you don't know where things are going. It's important to start this way. Otherwise, you risk being limited in community and vision.

- **Listen to people, but don't settle as the listener**
  Once you invite people to talk to you, you must listen. And listen with all of yourself. Really exercise your mind. Then, take the information you receive and get to work. Don't stay in the chair.

- **Engage.**
  Think, think, think. Talk, talk, talk. Be the verb!

[Name]

Agoranov

[Elevator Pitch]

"We are a leading science and tech incubator in Paris, supporting deep and frontier technologies. We work with talented founders and entrepreneurs that approach the market with an open mindset and innovative ideas."

[Sector]

All Sectors

[Description]

Among Paris entrepreneurial programs, Agoranov is by far the most chronicled. With fifteen years' experience and an outstanding track record, this program is a Paris startup institution. It has hosted over 320 startups, including five companies – among them Criteo – that were publicly listed on NASDAQ and forty that still work there now. "We were nearly the first on the scene. It was a bit more difficult, culturally speaking, to establish an incubation program in Paris ten or fifteen years ago, and we recognize we're a part of a world movement," says director Jean-Michel Dalle.

Located in the heart of Parisian academia, Agoranov shares with its accepted startups 2,300 m² of private offices, open workspaces, laboratories, fully equipped meeting rooms and a cafeteria. Open to startups from all sectors, the program trusts in the "lab" and classroom nature of business creation. As an incubator manager, Jean-Michel and his team want to help entrepreneurs investigate their surroundings and integrate into networks and markets. "But really, too, we play the role of sparring partner; in discussions, we oppose them so that they will know what dark corner to turn to next to truly realize their project and product," explains Jean-Michel. "The only one who can find solutions is the person, but we can be the environment, providing all the correct nutrients for life."

Typically accepting thirty applicants a year out of more than two hundred, Agoranov is uniquely dedicated to its members, providing, in addition to a home, training sessions, workshops with thought-leaders and experts, meetings with investors and connections with alumni. "Success, we believe, is always very individual in nature. Our startups have always succeeded in very different ways. What we do prescribe, however, is how not to fail. We help them accelerate while avoiding these pitfalls," says Jean-Michel.

[Apply to]

agoranov.com

[Links]   Website: **agoranov.com** Facebook: **Agoranov** Twitter: **@Agoranov_innov**

- **Have a founding team of two or three people**
Your team can include a maximum of one
French citizen.

- **Speak English**
The entire program takes place in English, so
communicating in English is a must.

- **Be in a creation or growth phase**
Startups can be in the project phase (not yet
legally founded) or founded abroad. Companies
that already have headquarters or subsidiaries
in France are not eligible.

- **Be willing to live in France for one year**
Founders must be ready to live in France for the
duration of the program (one year) and work on
their startup projects full time.

[Name]
French Tech Ticket

[Elevator Pitch]
"The French Tech Ticket is a one-year program to attract international startup talent to France, and the French Tech Visa is a fast track visa program for startup founders, tech talents and tech investors willing to join France."

[Sector]
All sectors

[Description]
La French Tech is a government-sponsored initiative and collective brand that aims to promote and support startups in France and beyond, as well as attract international startups into France. In order to assist the latter, the French Tech initiative created the French Tech Ticket: a competition aimed to help entrepreneurs launch their ideas and grow their businesses in France. "The idea is not only to attract talent in France, but also make it as easy as possible to join the ecosystems here," says the French Tech initiative director David Monteau. The French Tech Ticket program includes a forty-five- thousand-euro grant per startup to cover professional expenses, a twelve-month incubation period in one of its partner incubators, an accelerated and simplified process for obtaining residence permits for the entrepreneurs and their families, a series of master classes and a mentoring program, as well as a help desk to assist the winning entrepreneurs with administrative formalities.

Originally only held in Paris, the second French Tech Ticket program has been extended to the French Tech regional areas, organized by thematic and business areas, meaning that some forty-one incubators in France will host the seventy winning projects in 2017. In the two years the program has run to date, it has attracted over a 1,000 applications from more than a 100 countries; over 100 startups have been accepted. The French Tech Initiative will also launch the French Ticket Visa in 2017, ostensibly a limited number of fast-track visas. "We noticed after the first competition that the visa was one of the most important aspects for companies, so we decided to offer some to startups looking to work with a French company or join an incubator in France. It's also open to, say, a French VC fund recruiting a foreign investor or a foreign firm that decides to open a branch in France. They still have to fulfill the basic visa criteria of course, but the fast track process means things are much quicker and easier."

[Apply to]
frenchtechticket.com

- **Develop your network**
  You want to include not only other startups but also people in strategic positions such as VCs or company executives so that growth and visibility are possible.

- **Be inclusive**
  Establishing a multi-generational, diverse and mixed outlook is best and will open doors to all kinds of possibilities.

- **Think global**
  Don't define yourself just within your local ecosystem; think big from the beginning and invite an international vision.

- **Communicate on social media**
  You have to be visible from the get-go; take ownership of key terms, hashtags and current stories.

- **Speak up at international events**
  If we wish for more opportunities for women entrepreneurs, we must be visible and communicative. Initiate discussion, ask questions, challenge the norms.

The International au Féminin

[Name]

[Elevator Pitch]
"The International au Féminin is an international network and think tank that aims to influence the digital and technology industries and the women who work in them. It pursues its mission by working with an open mind, agility and diversity."

[Sector]
Digital transformation, social venture, innovation

[Description]
In 2013, when Cecile Delettre founded the International au Féminin, she wished to create a community for a voice that was missing within the startup community. "We are trying to encourage women to develop their startups, to help them and give them inspiration and the tools they need to make themselves visible to users as well as big companies and VCs," explains Cecile. Supporting members through conferences tailored to the female business experience, the International au Féminin network immerses its community in opportunities and events where women can gather to discuss and exchange around technology innovation and mobile digitalization ecosystems both in France and abroad. Fifty percent of its members work as CEOs, CDOs and CMOs in big companies, 40 percent of its founders are startup founders, and the other 10 percent hail from other backgrounds, making the association distinctly diverse. At its most elemental level, the International au Féminin aims to support startup founders and advocate for entrepreneurship and intrapreneurship opportunities within developing or established businesses.

Working in partnerships with other startups and leading companies in Europe, the US and Asia, the program provides a space for an essential element of the startup community: the perspective of the female entrepreneur. Past programming has included conferences and talks designed to open dialogue around innovation, "how to make the world a better place," the transition towards artificial intelligence and robotics. "We also organize workshops on developing skills that are critical to founding successful organizations, such as how to pitch, media training, attracting press interest and harnessing social media power," says Cecile. The program highlights women working in entrepreneurship in France, the US, Germany and beyond at events like the International Consumer Electronics Show, CeBIT, iMediaBrand Summit, Paris Retail Week and E-marketing Paris.

[Apply to]
cecile@internationalaufeminin.com

[Links]
Web: **intfem.com** Facebook: **siefeminin** Twitter: **@IntFem_**

- **Fall in love with the problem**
  Before building a solution, you have to be in love with the problem you want to solve. The more you focus on understanding the problem of your clients, the easier it will be to define a solution.

- **Make sure your market is big enough**
  VCs want to invest in large markets, and pivoting is easier in a bigger market.

- **Focus on one feature**
  An early-stage startup must find THE main feature that will bring 90 percent of the value of your product. Multiple features means you don't know the main pain of your client.

- **Draft go-to-market strategy**
  It's fine to not know exactly what your go-to-market is (SEO, influencers, events, cold calls, etc.), but the key is to define what you want to do to test and measure the success of each action.

[Name]

NUMA Paris

[Elevator Pitch]

"NUMA Paris is a three-month long acceleration intensive that helps startups to realize their solutions and raise venture capital. We empower mission-driven tech entrepreneurs to solve the global problems of 2030."

[Sector]

Education, health, energy, transportation, security, future of work

[Description]

Joining the NUMA hub means landing in a world of plenty, where community-based events, startup acceleration, coworking spaces and corporate innovation all merge together to celebrate a revision of the future. Numa's acceleration program aspires to engage startups that are thought-leaders. Its hands-on, three-month intensive program promises to "stress test" startups' execution plans. Once accepted, startups undergo three stages of coaching that ask them to question, fine-tune and execute their projects. "Execution is a key word of the program. We work with our startups to connect them with active mentors and venture capital, which complements the methodology we offer so they can realize their project efficiently," says managing director of acceleration Romain Cochet.

According to Romain, "Who is your customer?" is one of the most important questions for a startup, and one that his team pushes startups to answer before anything else. "We don't think raising money is success. The process of becoming ready to raise money is a success because it helps you understand your go-to-market, your product. And that goes back to understanding who your customer is and what his deep pain is," says Romain.

NUMA supports its accepted startups by putting them in front of potential customers and giving them access to strategic partners. By coordinating meetings with people both in-house and in the field, NUMA wants to engage startups and mentors in long-term relationships. "We arrange a match-day. The startups meet fifteen mentors in forty-eight hours. They could be CEOs, product owners or angel investors, but they're all active in the startup community and know what they are looking for. If a mentor and startup match, the startup will then be accompanied throughout their process," explains Romain.

[Apply to]

paris.numa.co

- **Have a clear vision**
  Know where you want to take your company from
  the very beginning. Identify your core values and
  be ready to share them.

- **Search for a team that you can trust and will
  challenge you**
  Your team should complete your own profile,
  from the technical to the sales side. You can't
  succeed alone!

- **Take time to precisely define your market**
  Identify all your potential customers, and know
  your competitors' strengths and weaknesses.
  It's important to understand what you bring to
  your customers.

- **Listen to your customers**
  Understand the need that your product or service
  fills, and what you bring that differentiates you
  from your competitors.

- **Fine-tune your business plan**
  You want to master your plan's execution in all
  aspects (recruitment, cash level, etc.), so have
  a clear vision of your next steps.

Paris&Co

[Name]

[Elevator Pitch]

"Paris&Co is the economic development and innovation agency of Paris. We run incubation programs for startups, facilitate cooperation with corporates and organize experimentation. Together with our partners, we stir the innovation ecosystem through the organization of events."

[Sector]

IT, smart city, tourism, smartfood, sports, healthcare, publishing

[Description]

Dedicated to fostering startup development, Paris&Co incubates emerging companies in a multitude of sectors. In 2016, more than 270 French and 30 international startups were nurtured in its programs. Comprised of nine innovation platforms, the agency aims to gather a complete ecosystem around the startups, thus structuring and facilitating collaborations with large corporate partners. "For more than twenty years now, the agency has never stopped reinventing itself – transforming from a pure incubation program to now including an innovation platform. We like to support our startups with multiple skillsets and a diversity of potential partners. We think of ourselves as a gateway for startups looking for more business opportunities, and we offer that with our network of international connections and expertise on open innovation," says Karine Bidart, co-CEO.

To build continuity and community around this idea, Paris&Co created the Open Innovation Club, which runs tailored, quarterly meetings between corporates and selected startups, themed "Innovation Dating" sessions and "Club Open Innovation" workshops on strategic subjects. The Urban Lab of Paris&Co helps companies field-test their prototypes and puts startups in real situations prior to market release.

These companies can benefit from unique connections with Paris's government and large corporates. "Since 2010, we have selected and supported over 300 projects and enabled 200 experiments in Paris, making it a hyperactive and dense playground for innovation in the city," explains Karine. "The Urban Lab initiatives really aim at improving city transport systems, fostering better use and management of natural resources, reducing Paris's environmental footprint, accelerating the energy transition, addressing climate change, developing the sharing and collaborative economy and encouraging social innovation for care and inclusion." Organizing more than 330 events annually, such as the Hacking of City Hall, an event that fosters business opportunities for startups, Paris&Co is reenvisioning the links between entrepreneurs, corporations, institutions and creative talent.

[Apply to]

parisandco.com

[Links]

Web: **parisandco.com** Facebook: **parisandcoagency** Twitter: **@Paris_and_Co**

- **Don't try to be perfect**
  Simple is better than perfect. Try something small and prove the concept.

- **Share your ideas and people will share with you**
  Talk about your idea from the very beginning because you will need to involve partners and developers as soon as possible. Don't be afraid to talk about your idea in its rough stages. If you don't start working on it with others, someone else will.

- **Find your mentors and find your partners**
  You need people helping you. Don't stay alone for years without partners. You will waste your time and endanger the life of your project.

- **Be obsessed with finding the right business model for your company**
  You need to build your community, but first you need a model – and funding will find you if you pay attention to structuring your company.

Paris Pionniéres

[Name]

[Elevator Pitch] *"We are the leading not-for-profit incubator for female entrepreneurs. Since 2005, we have launched 300 startups cofounded by women. As a result, Paris has become the European capital for gender diversity in tech with 21 percent women founders!"*

[Sector] **All sectors**

[Description] Created in March 2005, Paris Pionnières promotes the development of female entrepreneurs in the French and European landscape by offering not only a hub of inspiration but also three types of programming – Possible Camp, WoDi and Incubation. The directors of this program define their mission as changing the culture of startups: "The startup culture is a 'bro' culture. Women approach potential partners and investors who still subscribe to a certain skepticism in female leadership. We don't accept that. Through our programs and mentorship, we help female entrepreneurs incarnate their vision and express with confidence their ideas for innovation," explains managing director Caroline Ramade.

To prove its dedication to change in the startup ecosystem, Paris Pionnières is committed to several internal principles. First, it does not take any capital from the businesses it supports. Second, despite its mission to empower women, the program believes above all in diversity, and invites projects with mixed gender teams to join its spaces and workshops. Third, as best expressed by Caroline, "We want to find spaces that have not yet been opened. Our research and funding partnerships emerge from an interest in total innovation."

Out of 700 applications, Paris Pionnières' accelerator program, or WoDi, accepts forty new startups per year. While the competition is steep, accepted startups can expect individual and collective coaching from CEOs, CTOs and entrepreneurs in residence. "We concentrate on how to communicate your vision through digital tools and how to develop a business plan. We want to fill them up with confidence and to combat this Google search image of a Barbie CEO. We want all of our startups to know how to talk their numbers. Females can face a double standard in these situations. We're fighting that," says Caroline.

[Apply to] **pionnieres.paris.com**

[Links] Web: **pionnieres.paris** Facebook: **PionnieresParis** Twitter: **@ParisPionnieres**

- **Choose good entrepreneurs for your team**
  Do they have ambition, courage and mental
  flexibility? Are they friendly and creative enough
  to play with the rules to make something work?

- **Pick people who fit together**
  What does each founder bring to the table?
  Are they friends? Will they endure working
  together over the long run?

- **Keep an open but determined mindset**
  Sometimes you have to give before you get.
  Keep a "pay it forward" mentality. Determination is
  about the goal; openness is about the means.

- **Question yourself**
  Ask yourself, from many different angles,
  "Is the problem I'm trying to solve a real need?"

[Name]

TheFamily

[Elevator Pitch]

"TheFamily nurtures startups through education, unfair advantages and capital. We accompany startups on the long-run and for the long-term. Our mission is to educate entrepreneurs, build an infrastructure to empower them and build privileged access to smart investors."

[Sector]

Education, healthcare, finance, food, transportation

[Description]

Over the past four years, TheFamily has empowered over 500 startups, 220 of which are still active members in its network. Based in Paris, Berlin and London, this program does not believe in sectors, and holds that digital is intrinsic to any current business strategy. Though not an incubator, VC or accelerator, TheFamily, a self-proclaimed Black Swan Factory, is looking for true social innovation and for teams that are tackling issues that matter. "When we speak with startups, we want to ask them, is your project speaking to a real problem? A real need for a client? This is why we think education is so important, and why we welcome hard questions. Through this process we all learn, do-ers and startup teams alike," says CEO Alice Zagury.

Acting as a European platform wherein companies could envision raising funds in London, hiring in Paris, and executing in Berlin, TheFamily wants to help entrepreneurs scale beyond the traditional frameworks and networks. Trusting that the digital revolution has already sunk its teeth into communications and media, it is looking to the worlds that are falling behind, such as agriculture, healthcare, education and other public services. "We are there to make the pertinent introductions so that entrepreneurs can find the right investors while avoiding certain pitfalls. We provide the infrastructure so nobody drowns out there. If we are trying to do something totally new, we will guide it, like you would any new life," explains Alice.

Providing exclusive deals, including one with Amazon Web Services in Europe, as well as with IBM, Facebook, PayPal and Github, TheFamily saves its entrepreneurs money and time by giving them access to the most current services on the market. "We also arrange office hours for startups with our partners so that they can begin, early on, to establish independence. We love creating the relationship, this kind of tryst with reality from which the whole infrastructure benefits," says Alice.

[Apply to]

thefamily.co

[Links] Web: **thefamily.co** Facebook: **Welcome2TheFamily** Twitter: **@_TheFamily**

ces

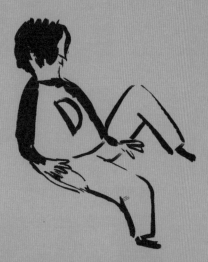

[Name] # Anticafé République

[Address] 6 rue de Château d'Eau, 75010 Paris

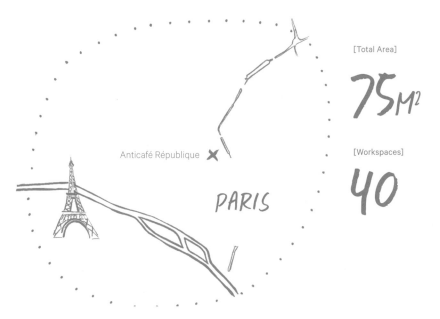

Anticafé République

PARIS

[Total Area]

75M²

[Workspaces]

40

[The Story] What started as a simple desire to create a cozy café where entrepreneurs could work has now expanded into a full European map of Anticafés. There are more than four locations in Paris proper, with the largest, Anticafé Beaubourg, featuring a robust sixty-five workstations, and there are plans for more in La Défense and Xavier Niel's Station F. Anticafé has also rolled out three more spaces in Aix en Provence, Lyon and Rome. "A presence in every major French city and an expansion in Europe was intended. I always wanted to build a greater international community and connect people," explains CEO and founder Leonid Goncharov.

The center of each Anticafé, as in so many homes, is the kitchen. There visitors and members can find a variety of snacks, fruits, cereals, drinks and salads. With three different layout styles, each Anticafé boasts options in terms of rooms, whether an individual wants some peace and privacy or a group wants to hunker down on some couches or around a more formal table. "It's becoming prestigious to be an entrepreneur, but it can be lonely, too," explains Leonid, "and we wanted to say, here is the space where we can work together in Europe."

Face of the Space:

"I chose entrepreneurship really early," says Leonid Goncharov, who began his career at just seventeen years old. After becoming frustrated with limited workspace options in Paris, Leonid decided to introduce an anti-Parisian model: "Entrepreneurs in Paris need space and community. At home in the Ukraine or even in Russia or the US, I could easily find cafés in which to spend hours and hours, but Paris lacked this."

[Name] # DRAFT Ateliers

[Address] 12 Espl. Nathalie Sarraute, 75018 Paris

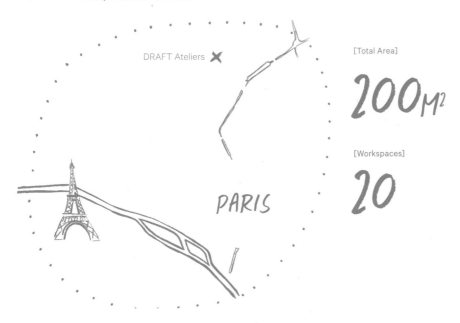

DRAFT Ateliers ✈

PARIS

[Total Area]

200M²

[Workspaces]

20

[The Story] In the ever-changing ecosystem of Paris, there are coworking spaces and there are cocreation spaces. Three years ago, Anne Gautier and Quentin Billey looked around their city and felt something was missing. "Everything is devoted to tech innovation, but we wanted to provide product designers and artists with a space to create and sell," says Anne, cofounder of DRAFT Ateliers. Inspired by makerspaces in the US, these two young ex-e-commerce professionals wanted to make a brand new French workshop: "We wanted to bring this to France, to Paris; it didn't exist. When we launched DRAFT, we were one of two launching at the same time. But then we saw this whole market develop. It was definitely in the air; we couldn't ignore it," says Anne.

The 200 m² that is DRAFT are composed of two studios, with its chief purpose to give makers a space and to encourage collaboration and method-sharing. In addition, Anne and Quentin hope makers will choose to sell within the workshops to continue the life cycle of the space. These moments of community are some of the most important for Anne: "I love it when I see people collaborating, when a project meets another one, when people are exchanging methods. To see people holding their first prototype in their hands is a magic moment."

[Links]   Web: ateliers-draft.com Facebook: draftateliers Twitter: @draftateliers Instagram: draftateliers

Face of the Space:

Anne Gautier studied political science at Écoles de hautes études politiques, where she specialized in political communication before starting work with the creation collective 9th Concept. Always a serigraph artist at heart, Anne worked at the Centre Pompidou and venteprivee.com before opening DRAFT Ateliers with Quentin in 2014.

[Name] # Kwerk

[Address]   44–46 rue de la Bienfaisance, 75008 Paris

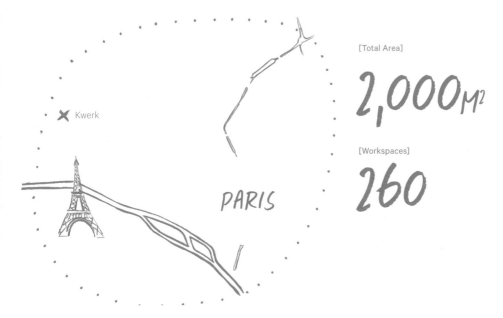

[Total Area]

2,000M²

[Workspaces]

260

Kwerk

PARIS

[The Story]   Kwerk, from "quirky", meaning characterized by unexpected traits, is a coworking, cobreathing space dedicated to hosting an uplifting vibe. "We wanted to bring this quirkiness to our space, to invite people who lived '*à l'ouest,*' which in French describes people who are a bit different, who don't go with the norm," says cofounder Lawrence Knights.

In fact, wellness is the centerpiece of Kwerk, and those joining its "flow" will find space to both work and practice yoga, meet deadlines and de-stress. Unlike other coworking spaces in the city, Kwerk Bienfaisance, along with three other spacious locations in the city, invites you to stick around for a lot more than just "working" hours. "We have showers, changing rooms, a proper training room. All of this. After our living in the East, we came back to Paris with a need to put a lot of oneness into this metropolis. We hope we've created a little haven." Lawrence opened Kwerk with his associate and life partner Albert Angel, and the two have curated the place to embody the safe havens they knew in their nomadic past. "We gave it a fun and approachable design, featuring custom-made pieces from around the world. We keep the space in motion and alive with changing installations because we want people to project themselves into the space," explains Lawrence.

[Links]   Web: kwerk.fr Facebook: kwerkcoworking Twitter: @kwerk_FR Instagram: kwerkparis

Face of the Space:

Lawrence Knights grew up "à l'ouest" in the suburbs of Paris. After attending HEC, he found himself unhappy in the consulting and banking world. Taking time to travel, Lawrence found a love for Eastern aesthetics during his years spent in Bali and Jakarta.

[Name] # Le Laptop

[Address] 6 rue Arthur Rozier, 75019 Paris

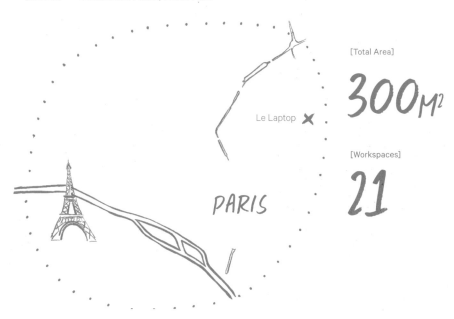

[Total Area]

300m²

[Workspaces]

21

Le Laptop ✗

PARIS

[The Story] The idea behind Le Laptop is simple, yet still not easily achievable in a bustling metropolis like Paris. Tucked away in the quieter, less touristic 19th arrondissement is an intimate coworking space where freelancers and nomad workers can congregate for both work and workshops. Launched in 2012 by artist and designer Pauline Thomas, Le Laptop is distinctly tied to the idea of collaboration, and that's how the space maintains its supportive, invitational feel, requiring no application and turning down no wandering innovator.

"We can host twenty people. It's quite intimate. And that's important to us, that you're known, that you have a name, that people communicate and on a real level," says Pauline. Le Laptop focuses on cordial privacy and communal spaces – private desks, meeting rooms and a big kitchen allowing guests to lunch together. As an added bonus, Pauline and her community develop weekly and monthly workshops within the space for entrepreneurs and other businesses that focus on UX design: "It's like a mini-school. We have a training program to teach companies, freelancers and startups the techniques and methods needed for creating a better product and user experience from earliest conception." That space and education mix is essential to the mission of Le Laptop, a home that seeks to enable and empower Paris's creative minds.

[Links] Web: lelaptop.com Facebook: LeLaptop Twitter: @Le_Laptop Instagram: le_laptop

Face of the Space:
Founder Pauline Thomas is an artist, photographer and expert UX designer. Pauline wishes to share her experience from Google and Adobe and provide a comfortable space for other innovators. "I always felt it was a pity to be in a city with so much potential but no way to access your community, so I discovered places, spaces in New York, in San Francisco, that showed me what we could do in Paris."

[Name] # Le Loft 50 Partners

[Address] 62 rue Jean-Jacques Rousseau, 75001 Paris

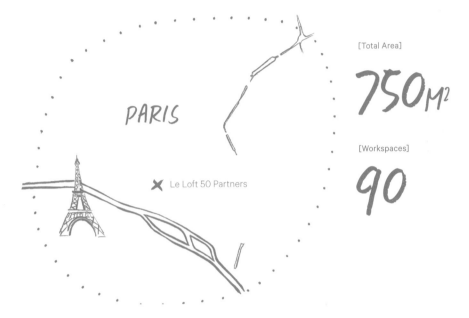

PARIS

✕ Le Loft 50 Partners

[Total Area]

750M²

[Workspaces]

90

[The Story] Le Loft, which refers to the physical address of 50 Partners, nourishes Paris's most promising startups. Established in July 2012, Le Loft is a unique community of fifty successful serial entrepreneurs that want to build and give a home to the startup ecosystem of Paris. "Our wish is to gather around us and to give life to the great minds of the Paris startup environment," says Virginie Augagneur, events and operation manager of Le Loft 50 Partners. To ensure that the space feels charged not only with independence for startups but also with community, Le Loft hosts several weekly and monthly events – community breakfasts, pitch projects and the famous "Apéroft" (a combination of the French "apéro" and "loft") – to stimulate innovation, growth and camaraderie in their offices, located in the heart of Les Halles.

Unlike many other spaces in the city, Le Loft's members, those accepted into the 50 Partners program, are granted full access to this exquisite converted coworking and event space. "We are a long-life incubator because we are focused on the fact that help and expertise does not expire in six months but must continue through all stages, at growth and international expansion. We want to see exponential growth, and we believe that happens in environments of accessibility and stability, thus Le Loft," explains Virginie.

[Links] Web: 50partners.fr/Ecosysteme/Le-loft Facebook: 50Partners Twitter: @50partners

Face of the Space:

Virginie Augagneur, originally from Brittany, migrated to the startup world after receiving her degree from business school and spending many years in the hospitality and catering industry. Now, Virginie devotes her days to animating Le Loft: "What I love to see is when two people meet who have never met, and you just know they've found each other, they've made a lasting connection. It's really what we do; why we are here."

[Name] # Liberté Living-Lab

[Address] 9 rue d'Alexandrie, 75002 Paris

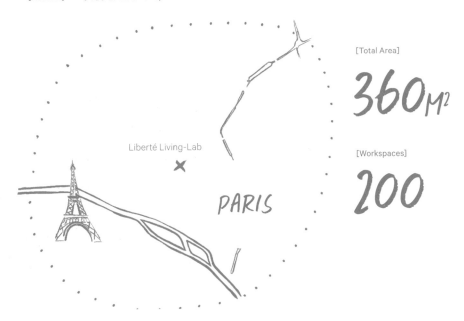

[Total Area]

360M²

[Workspaces]

200

Liberté Living-Lab

PARIS

[The Story] After months of experimentation in coworking spaces in Paris, Liberté Living-Lab (LLL) cofounders Jérôme Richez and Marylène Vicari wanted to invest their leadership experience and skill sets in a venture that would help crystallize tech, civic and social innovation. Following its first incarnation, Player, LLL opened in October 2016. LLL seeks to bring people, projects and teams from diverse backgrounds together in the same place. "We are home to just as many artists as we are data scientists, programmers and corporations," says comanager Mohammed Adnène Trojette.

LLL is already host to Hello Tomorrow, Data for Good, Bayes Impact, Jam and Lab School Network, and supports a diverse calendar of public events, such as Artificial Intelligence and Smart Cities, Positive Impact Investing, and Health and Transportation. While LLL is careful in selecting its residents, it does not, unlike many coworking spaces and incubators in Paris, take equity. "We believe in the independence of our residents. Part of their job is working on resolution, using technological methods that could apply to public interest, like solving challenges around unemployment, reassessing strategies in public education and implementing resources for refugees. We want them to be free to explore. It's in our name," explains Adnène.

[Links] Web: **liberte.paris** Facebook: **liberte.paris** Twitter: **@LIBERTE_LL**

Face of the Space:

After receiving his engineering degree from Centrale Paris and a master's in public affairs from Sciences Po and finishing the École nationale d'administration, Mohammed Adnène Trojette became a civil servant. His commitment to justice in the public sector through digital problem solving and innovation led him to join Liberté Living-Lab as comanager in November 2016.

[Name] # Nuage Café

[Address] 14 rue des Carmes, 75005 Paris

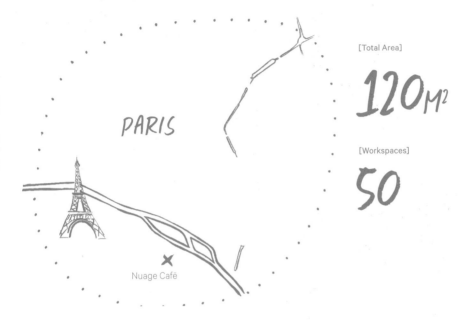

[Total Area]

120m²

[Workspaces]

50

PARIS

Nuage Café

[The Story] In 2015 Emmanuel and Benjamin Watrinet, twin brothers, were living the corporate lifestyle but longing for the intimacy of a family business. The idea was still amorphous, so they took to coffee shops to discuss it: "We were looking for simple things – a strong Wi-Fi connection, office equipment, a wide range of operating hours, ambiance. But we couldn't find this. We were always forced into places like Starbucks, where it was noisy and chaotic. We thought, this is crazy; there's no place for us to work after hours," says Benjamin, manager and COO.

Thus Nuage Café was born. Once the high school of Cyrano de Bergerac and more recently a Dominican convent, Nuage, which means "cloud" in French, is true to its name: a tranquil duplex featuring various shared and private work environments. Hoping to host a new coworking atmosphere, these brothers chose this name to maintain a connected lightness. "We saw other meanings, too. There is the metaphorical 'nuage' of café au lait, or the English homophone of 'new age.' We just wanted to announce ourselves as different, as a calm space," says Benjamin. In-house services include drinks and snacks, fast Wi-Fi, books, newspapers, a piano and games. Members of Nuage can book their spaces online and network with other freelancers, startups, writers and students who want to work in a unique culture.

[Links] Web: **nuagecafe.fr** Facebook: **NuageCafeParis** Twitter: **@_NuageCafe** Instagram: **cafenuage**

Face of the Space:
Benjamin Watrinet is manager and
COO of Nuage Café. As head barista
and best friend to all Nuage members,
Benjamin wears many hats, but is gripped
by one obsession: to put every coworker
on cloud nine. Previously a consultant
for Ernst & Young, Benjamin loves the
upstairs of Nuage, a little cocoon he
describes as a cozy "poof" under a
vaulted ceiling filled with natural light.

[Name] # Partech Shaker

[Address] 33 rue du Mail, 75002 Paris

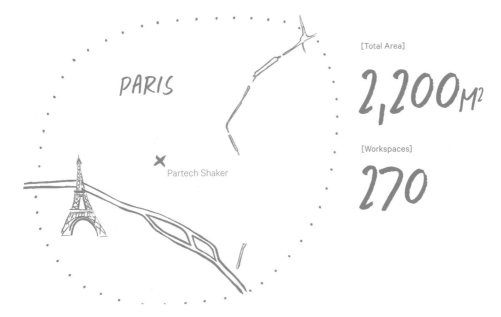

PARIS

Partech Shaker

[Total Area]

*2,200*M²

[Workspaces]

270

[The Story] Partech Shaker is the first initiative from a venture capital firm dedicated to the local Parisian ecosystem. Opened in 2014 by the international VC firm Partech Ventures, this startup campus is located in the heart of the city's technology district and boasts 2,200 m² and space for thirty teams, all within its pristine, design-hip nine stories. "We want to help our residents during their hyper-growth periods, times when they usually encounter their first-round challenges in funding, in finding a home, in building and expanding their business models and in hiring the best talents," says managing director Marie Raichvarg.

With partners including a network of international companies, local universities and business experts, and offering flexible, all-inclusive office spaces, the campus opens its doors and shares its networks with ambitious, business-ready startups from all over the world, not solely those backed by Partech Ventures. Global leaders such as Amazon, Stripe, Braintree and Microsoft make up a part of Partech Shaker's rich and perk-filled community. In 2016, the campus launched a soft-landing solution – Europe Made Easy – a house-crafted tool available to each of its resident startups. Next year, Partech Shaker will initiate the first French Techstars acceleration program, attracting even more international companies to the campus, which already counts among its residents Dropbox, Pinterest, Made.com, Hired and Kantox.

[Links] Web: partechshaker.com Facebook: PartechShaker Twitter: @PartechShaker

Face of the Space:

Marie Raichvarg joined Partech Ventures as managing director of the startup campus in 2014. She transitioned into the startup world seamlessly, as her work in the media industry had positioned her at the heart of Paris's digital revolution. "At some point, I discovered the world of entrepreneurship, and I really became attracted to this world, its energy and ambition. When I finally met Partech, it was like we chose each other."

[Name] Station F

[Address] 55 Boulevard Vincent-Auriol, 75013 Paris

PARIS

Station F ✈

[Total Area]

3,400M²

[Workspaces]

3,000

[The Story] "We want this to be an international community and to make entrepreneurship available to anybody, regardless of education and background," says Roxanne Varza, director of Station F. Station F provides an inclusive and multifaceted space, boasting 3,000 workstations, 8 event spaces, a 360-seat auditorium, 4 kitchens, a bar open 24/7 and plans to incorporate a housing component in the next year. Announcing itself as the largest startup campus in the world – it's literally as long as the Eiffel Tower is tall – Station F symbolizes French entrepreneur Xavier Niel's 250-million-euro investment in the international startup culture. "He loves big ambitious projects. He loves serving under-served communities and building community where it feels non-existent. Today, the Parisian startup ecosystem isn't as international as that of London, Berlin or Silicon Valley, but we are working to change that," says Roxanne.

Already welcoming 1,000 startups and fifteen to twenty programs, including its in-house "Founders Program," Station F promises a community of resources and support for startups as they forge their path and their network. "In the Founders Program, we give startups liberty. They have complete independence and will even have private meeting rooms where they can invite prospective partners, investors, et cetera," says Roxanne.

[Links] Web: **stationf.co** Facebook: **STATIONF** Twitter: **@joinstationf** Instagram: **joinstationf**

Face of the Space:

Originally from San Francisco, Roxanne Varza worked for two years for the French government's foreign direct investment agency assisting American startups in France. After meeting Xavier Niel while working for TechCrunch, Roxanne says it was a simple reply to an email that began the vision of Station F: "He wrote me asking my thoughts on the project. I wrote him back with a list of ideas, he invited me to meet with architects. Then, all of the sudden, we were creating this campus."

Martin Duval
/ bluenove

Founder and President

"I started bluenove in 2008, but I still see my company as a startup," says bluenove founder and president Martin Duval. "We are forty people now and our business is open innovation and collective intelligence for public and private organizations – that is, helping major corporations to become open organizations as a culture and show them how to work better with startups and form collaborations with the stakeholders of their ecosystem."

Before founding bluenove, Martin headed up different management positions in innovation and business development at Orange, an experience he said laid the foundations for his company. "My job at Orange was to make the company more active in terms of open innovation, finding the best ways to identify, select and partner with innovative startups. That not only gave me the experience but also the will and insight to start a brand that could capture what I believed was the beginning of a strong trend for big corporations and organizations needing external innovative partners such as startups." That vision has been proved entirely correct not only by the growth of bluenove (100 percent over the last two years) but also that of the markets within France and worldwide. A large turning point for the company was teaming up with a Montreal-based software company whose collective intelligence platform, Assembl, now lies at the heart of bluenove's services.

"Assembl was more of an R&D project that at that time was part of a European Commission project on how to build a European Constitution," says Martin. "The challenge was how to collect new information and knowledge from thousands of people within a short time period. I realized that their solution was a good methodology for open innovation in general, especially as it works well with both corporate and civic projects. It really helps us and the companies we work with disrupt traditional strategy planning, whether it's aiding corporations to tackle issues in a very collaborative way or the French government recently recommending us as a reliable civictech."

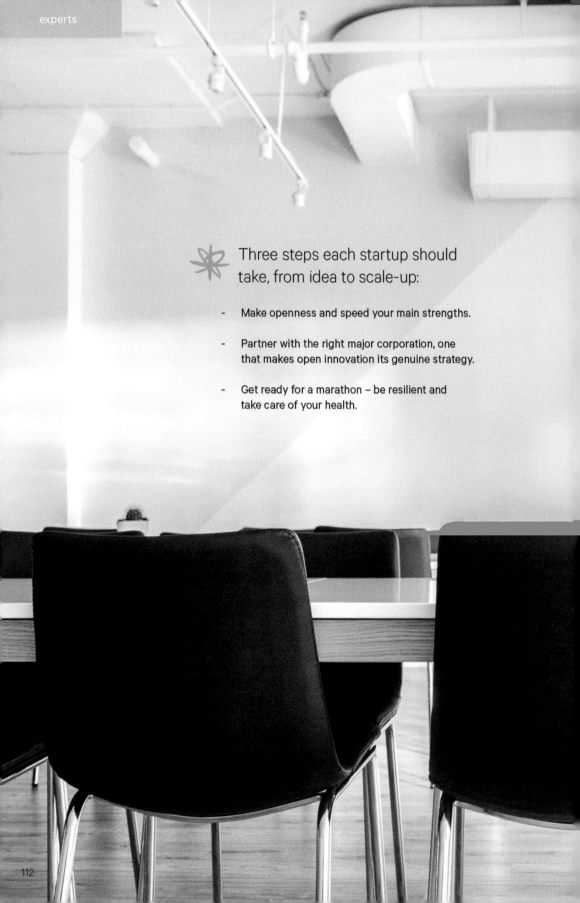

Three steps each startup should take, from idea to scale-up:

- Make openness and speed your main strengths.

- Partner with the right major corporation, one that makes open innovation its genuine strategy.

- Get ready for a marathon – be resilient and take care of your health.

Dos & Don'ts:

Do create and keep passion in your team.

Do make resilience your key quality.

Do think of your project as part of an ecosystem of stakeholders.

Don't hide your ideas – share them all, test many, fail fast and focus on what's left.

Don't underestimate your intuition, you are an entrepreneur.

Don't hesitate to merge your private passions with your professional ones.

Not satisfied with being the first consultancy to have an integrated software solution designed specifically to support collective intelligence with very large groups of people, bluenove is currently underlining its agile mindset and flexible structure by switching its baseline from open innovation to open organizations, a way to support the evolution of how people manage collaborations and external innovation partners. To do this, it is even hiring a former client. "We did a study a few weeks ago to measure the evolution of relationships between startups and corporations, which consisted of three things. One was speed, which big organizations are still trying to tackle. The second was simplicity, which draws on the lean startup approach to help bigger companies work differently, and the third is benevolence, which was based around constructive sharing and trust – a very big challenge for large companies, but also for startups, which used to be frightened about having ideas stolen, et cetera. The overall results of the study were very optimistic for the future. We have found that there is more openness and trust overall, which creates a strong foundation for everyone to build on. As someone who began as an evangelist, it's very satisfying to see this maturity of the market and new and more open kinds of leadership emerging."

Case Studies

bluenove is the project manager behind the 2017 Spark Life Contest, a European competition that enables a selected community of corporations to get together and find, select and support startups. The six sponsors are Sodexo, Accor Hotels, Steelcase, SNCF, thecamp and Le Village, and the main theme is quality of life, which is broken down into three categories: health and wellbeing, space and environment, and social interaction. Following an inaugural event in Paris, the event was presented in key cities around Europe. "Our job is to get the six corporate sponsors efficiently aligned and agreeing," says Martin Duval. "We believe that competitions tlike this should be the future of working and managing innovation, because it's not only about a lump sum of money given to a startup but a great chance to win a contract with a corporation. And even if the startup doesn't win, or even if it isn't mature enough, it will probably get some kind of opportunity, visibility or insight. Ultimately it's an acceleration platform for business development and partnership opportunities."

At bluenove, we support a new breed of leadership and performance for open organizations that believe in societal impact and competitive advantage through their ability to better manage the innovation and collective intelligence of the stakeholders of their ecosystem.

Albert Asséraf / JCDecaux France

Executive VP of Strategy, Data and User Innovation

Number one out-of-home advertising company worldwide, JCDecaux was founded in 1964 by Jean-Claude Decaux. Specializing in street furniture, transport advertising and billboards, the company today operates in over seventy-five countries, reaches over four hundred million people in the world every day and has long been a major player in the global startup ecosystem, working with Les Grands Prix de l'Innovation in Paris and more recently entering a partnership with Toucan Toco, a company that develops apps based on big data. The company has also run its own incubators in the past, notably with Paris&Co for the Services Urbains Connectés business incubator, a two-year program started in 2013 in which three different startups – Aerys, Park24 and TellMePlus – worked on projects from intelligent car parks to targeted digital adverts connected to street furniture. It also operated a six-month acceleration project with BNP Paribas' Innov&Connect program in 2016, which spawned collaboration with Paris startup Diduenjoy to conduct quick-turnaround surveys to identify trends and get fast feedback on mobility projects such as bike-sharing.

The company tends to meet with around two or three startups a week, and holds constant meetings with VCs and specialists to identify and map out opportunities within the company's main fields – smart city, sustainable mobility, digital advertising and the Internet of Things. With around 160 engineers based in Paris and 13,000 employees worldwide, the company is also thinking of developing its own in-house startup culture. "We think it's time to work differently," says Albert Asséraf, executive VP of strategy, data and user innovation at JCDecaux. "To organize an open innovation program on one side and continue developing innovation within our company on the other, and connect these two elements. We are a very integrated company in general, and do many things internally, but things move so fast that open innovation is now relevant. For example, the next generation of sustainable mobility will involve battery-operated electric bicycles, so we are seeking startups working in this area. On the advertising side there are many operations to consider too. We have 50,000 digital billboards operating in cities across the globe, so real-time advertising is a major topic for us – but we also know that these cities are encouraging citizen participation through digital assets. Startups that can analyze conversations on social media and web and mobile behaviors are also important for us as a way of finding a new generation of audience measurement."

Dos & Don'ts:

[
Do carefully choose your first team members, they're the ones who'll grow your business.

Do test and learn with actual clients to perfect your solution.

Do surround yourself with experienced mentors to fast-track your business.
]

[
Don't hesitate to pivot when necessary.

Don't lose track of your core objective and unique selling proposition.

Don't give up! If there's a market for your business idea, go for it.
]

Three steps each startup should
take, from idea to scale-up:

- Concentrate on making your product or solution perfect.

- Partner with key clients who will bring increased visibility
and credibility to your company.

- Work at it, work at it and work at it again; it's not the great
idea that's the most important, it's what you make of it.

Case Studies

In 2016, JCDecaux partnered with Diduenjoy, a startup specializing in mobile-first client feedback, to cocreate an innovative way to interact with JCDecaux's bike-sharing clients. tJCDecaux worked hand in hand with Diduenjoy to bring the three-month-long pilot live, which more than a thousand clients then used to share feedback on their trips and the state of the bikes they had just used – all in less than ten seconds, thanks to a custom-built interface. Since this first collaboration, Diduenjoy has gone on to develop its business with e-commerce startups like Cheerz as well as large companies such as LVMH. "We were impressed with JCDecaux's reactivity and startup state of mind," says Diduenjoy cofounder Louis de Froment, "which made it really easy to interface our system with their IT infrastructure. For us, it was all the more beneficial as we have been able to use the developments we made for JCDecaux with other clients."

To make its media offers and argumentation easier and more digital, JCDecaux worked with Toucan Toco, a dataviz startup that was founded in 2014 to give companies broader access to their performance data to add value to their decision-making. Toucan Toco offers small applications that are able to analyze, correlate and visualize sales, human resources, marketing and financial data through mobile devices. JCDecaux worked with it to empower its sales and marketing teams with a small app that encapsulates all solutions in a mobile-first interface. Beyond dataviz, Toucan Toco develops data storytelling for its clients. "Accessing our media anywhere, everywhere and on any device helps transform the way we do business with brands and media agencies."

[Contact] Tel: **+ 33 (0) 1 30 79 79 79**

[Links] Web: **jcdecaux.com** Facebook: **JCDecaux** Twitter: **@jcdecaux_france**

" We think it's time to work differently – to organize an open innovation program on one side and continue developing innovation within our company on the other, and connect these two elements. "

David Monteau
/ La French Tech

Director

La French Tech is the term used for the French startup ecosystem, as well as the name of a government initiative launched in 2013 to support the growth of this ecosystem. "The starting point was to provide support to the promising and expanding ecosystem in France," says the initiative's director David Monteau. "We saw the strong potential to go even further and wanted to support it. We know Paris well, of course, but other French cities have plenty of startups and talent, so we thought it would be interesting to network and boost the momentum. The initiative's role is purely to encourage the dynamics between the private actors, so we don't interfere in the business side." Another main aim is to connect the French to international ecosystems and address a somewhat unfair misperception of France as lagging behind in terms of innovation culture. "France has long been a paradise to start a business in the tech and biotech sectors, as there are so many tech talents, infrastructures, incubators and investors, and therefore support everywhere. The French Tech ecosystem is a global leader in a few sectors such as deeptech, healthtech and hardware, and we wanted to show that France is both an eager early adopter of technological innovation – even in terms of companies such as Uber or Airbnb, which have been widely accepted – and the birthplace of many scaleups bringing these innovations to the market."

To support this network and to facilitate connections between existing communities, the French Tech initiative has reached out to French startups operating around the globe – not just in San Francisco, New York and London but also in Africa, Brazil, China and beyond – to form informal networks of support and communication. This global network currently features around 500 startups across twenty-two cities.

Dos & Don'ts:

Do network. Our startup ecosystem has many players that regularly organize meetups (in English and in French).

Do try to get a grasp on French business etiquette. Lunchtime is sacred in France, but it's also a great time to do business.

Do reach out to investment funds, because Paris is full of them.

Don't take offense when the French are a bit late to meetings; it is not a sign of disrespect.

Don't despair when processes like opening a bank account or finding an apartment take longer than you expected – you will eventually succeed!

Don't hesitate to ask people to speak English if you do not understand French; most French do speak English – they're just a little self-conscious about their accent.

Three steps each startup should
take, from idea to scale-up:

- Reach out to investment funds – 85 percent of seed
  rounds for Parisian startups came from local investors,
  well above the global average of 70 percent.

- Think global right from the beginning. Have the ambition
  to be an international startup as opposed to focusing
  on a single market.

- Network. Sometimes a few good connections can
  make all the difference.

"The Parisian ecosystem is also much more international than it was even just five years ago," says David. "We see more and more startup meetups happening in English, which makes sense as more international talent is integrating into the French startup ecosystem." To boost this global dynamic, the French Tech initiative has organized the French Tech Ticket program along with the French Tech Visa to welcome international startups, entrepreneurs, investors and other tech talent to France. "As Philippe Botteri of Accel Partners confirmed, France has been the fastest growing startup ecosystem in Europe over the past five years," says David. "I think we can see from general growth and related statistics how much the startup economy has moved forward. We can also see the phenomenon in the evolving mindset of young people: the majority of young adults now want to found or work in startups. This is a big change in French society, and one that has been accelerating dramatically in the last few years."

The French Tech initiative now includes a new program called "French Tech Diversity" to detect and accompany talented startups with founders from socially diverse backgrounds. "The number of private accelerators and incubators has increased tremendously in the past three years, too," says David. "The launch of Station F, which is really the incarnation of the startup ecosystem and the arrival of international players such as Techstars demonstrate this. Large corporations in France have also realized the importance of the startup ecosystem and are increasingly investing in and finding ways of collaborating with startups. Of course, there can still be restrictions from the legal side, but it's normal for society to move faster than the government – which it must be said has been adapting very fast in the last years to foster entrepreneurship in the French economy." David and the French Tech Team are convinced that the new generation of successful startups at the global level will lean heavily on deeptech (AI, data, biotech, etc.). "Paris is very well positioned in this respect, as France is world-renowned for the quality of its engineers and now has an ecosystem that will allow these startups to grow and become world leaders."

"

Europe's tech scene is multi-centric, based on several highly interconnected, world-class startup centers with a wide but differentiated range of assets. With its deeptech startups and talents, a great density of VC funding and a proven capacity to build innovative business models, Paris is among Europe's top startup hotspots.

"

Stéphanie Hospital / OneRagtime

Cofounder and CEO

OneRagtime was founded in 2016 by Stéphanie Hospital and former Vivendi CEO Jean-Marie Messier. Stéphanie had previously been working at French multinational telecommunications corporation Orange, managing the digital business team and making acquisitions and partnerships with large tech players and early-stage startups. "I had the feeling I was doing so much for entrepreneurs that in the end I wanted to be one," says Stéphanie. "I founded OneRagtime precisely to give entrepreneurs what they need – not only money but also experience, access to corporations and the ability to scale quickly to an international level." The company is disrupting the traditional funding model with its studio for acceleration and partnership with leading investment bank Messier Maris & Associés, but it's also a unique venture platform that can quickly spot suitable startup talent and enable fast and effective funding and scaling through on-demand investments. Startups are able to register easily via their smartphones, and can then be analyzed and tracked through the platform's deep-dive screening tools, which assess suitability for funding and future matchmaking.

Accredited investors can back multiple entrepreneurs alongside a Top Tier VC, manage portfolios and keep track of investments all in one place. Accepted startups, usually those helping to disrupt the consumer realms of software and deep technology, get access to funds – anything from twenty-five thousand to a few million euros – as well as a well-rounded international team based in New York, London, Barcelona and Paris, and a mix of enthusiastic, tech-savvy millennials and older, more experienced business people. "I always felt there is a generation gap in the startup industry and this was our way of addressing it," says Stéphanie. "We want to bring together the best of these two worlds – young and hungry developers and disrupters looking for opportunities and a network of mentors and close advisors with experience in the tech industry as well as the corporate world."

Dos & Don'ts:

Do surround yourself with a great team comprised of people you really like.

Do select your investors carefully as you will be backed by them for a long time.

Do triple the time you think it will take to develop your company.

Don't bullshit people; you need to be transparent and honest in all your dealings.

Don't try to be overly sophisticated at the beginning – keep it simple.

Don't rush when hiring people and remember that the best talent continues to attract the best people.

Three steps each startup should take, from idea to scale-up:

- Think big but act small.

- Stay focused on developing an operation with technical capabilities that will help you to scale.

- Think hard about distribution; leverage the power of cooperation to distribute.

Despite the company's impressive digitization, personal chemistry remains of paramount importance to Stéphanie and the team. "We look for entrepreneurs and teams that are exceptional and that we can really build a great relationship with," she says. "We don't want companies to think we are just bringing money – we want coaching and development throughout, which means not just early-stage but Series A and B, right up to private equity and acquisition. We ask questions such as: Do we like the people within the company? Do they have something special? Do we want to spend time with them? In the same way we are always looking for investors who share the same values as us, who want the thrill of helping companies develop and bringing new innovation that can maybe also bring positive change to the world."

Case Studies

Founded in 2016 by young serial entrepreneurs Michael Philippe and Robin Sabban, Kelinetwork creates short form videos that are distributed through social media platforms. The company has successfully developed, from scratch, four leading channel verticals: Ohmygoal (soccer), Gamology (video games), Genius Club (innovation) and Beauty Studio (health and beauty). In the span of a few months, the channels have already amassed, in aggregate, over 600 million monthly video views, 50 million engaged users and 9 million fans. Every channel vertical is also number one or two in monthly video views within its respective category on Facebook. The development team is based in France, and the business and sales are led from New York.

Leveraging its proprietary portfolio of technology and one-of-a-kind social distribution expertise, Kelinetwork is perfectly positioned to disrupt the status-quo of the traditional media landscape. With the proper support and through its unique ability to scale, both on existing and new verticals, the company can quickly become the number one social channel player globally. "OneRagtime is one of the very few investors able to both challenge and support founders on the operational part of the business," says cofounder and CEO Michael Philippe. "They're pushing us to think global and their corporate expertise allows them to be much more than a traditional VC." OneRagtime is now leveraging its network in the US and unique partnership with an investment bank to back Kelinetwork in its next phase of development with a two-digit fund raised with strategic partners.

[Contact]   Email: **stephanie@oneragtime.com**

[Links]   Website: **oneragtime.com** Facebook: **oneragtime** Twitter: **@OneRagtime** Snapchat: **oneragtime**

"*We love consumer-type solutions and we want to invest in teams that are international and can build deeptech platforms that have the ability to disrupt.*"

Geoffroy Schmitt
/ PwC Startup Program

Transformation, Change and Innovation Leader, PwC France and
French-speaking Africa

The PwC France startup program caters to startups' needs throughout their journeys
towards success. It comprises DIVN (pronounce "dive in"), an incubation program created
for early-stage startups; an accelerator for more mature startups (PwC Accelerator); and
Smart Up, a wider initiative that offers the usual PwC services (accountants, lawyers and
consultants) at the right price for startups. "We started DIVN in 2016 for early-stage
startups that have just an idea or proof of concept but no revenue," says Geoffroy Schmitt,
transformation, change and innovation leader with PwC France. "Fifteen startups each
year get a coworking space in our campus-style offices, access to our internal experts
to answer questions on a variety of topics like cybersecurity, IP law, data science and
UX design, and business models and business plans. Our external partners also provide
professional help with some of the things we cannot do ourselves – such as how to run
a successful viral marketing campaign." DIVN also offers coaching, as well as help with
essential topics like customer acquisition.

The company's accelerator program – which predates DIVN by a year – is also attractive.
Designed for more mature startups and scaleups, it aims to push exponential growth and
globalization. "It's about firming up and refining processes and internationalizing companies
throughout the 150 countries where we are present," says Geoffroy. "We also help companies
raise funds and refine their strategy." The program also helps large companies designing
their own accelerator programs, and even sources promising startups to work with.

The Smart Up initiative is unique in that it offers PwC across-the-board services specifically
tailored to startups' needs in terms of price and delivery, from the optimal legal setup of a
new company, bookkeeping and tax services to protection of intellectual property, financing
(including via IPO) and auditing financial statements. "Much of our work in the innovation field
directly benefits us too," explains Geoffroy. "Working with startups helps us identify ways of
improving the way we work and serve our clients not only through technology but by
embedding innovative and entrepreneurial culture. Making sure we are agile is a priority, and
one of the ways we do that is to make sure we stay close to the startup ecosystem."

Three steps each startup should
take, from idea to scale-up:

- Plan for scale from the beginning; build robust
  processes and leverage the right corporate partners.

- Build a culture fostering execution; test and learn
  and pursue continuous improvements.

- Outsource your pain points to experienced
  professionals; cheap is more costly in the long run.

Dos & Don'ts:

Do find a problem that is worth solving and you are passionate about. Dream big!

Do build a team that is diverse, competent, works well together and is dedicated to a vision.

Do focus on bringing your end customers the best possible experience and generating revenues.

Don't lose sight of the core values you stand for. Make sure your team adheres to them.

Don't let roadblocks stall your projects. Find creative workarounds and be relentless.

Don't work in a silo. Build a community, network, communicate and be visible.

Case Studies

One of the startups PwC France has worked with is Uptime, a company that is disrupting the elevator maintenance industry via a connected object that's placed in elevators and sends alerts when there are problems. These alerts come with detailed information that helps technicians bring the right tools and parts. The next challenge for Uptime is predictive maintenance: using deep data analysis, it aims to be able to not only identify elevator problems but also determine when they will happen in advance. After meeting PwC in a pitch session, Uptime joined the incubation program, where it received coaching and advice on how to present its business plan to investors and was introduced to the right lawyer to design its IP strategy; it was also able to run a pilot with one of PwC's real estate clients. "DIVN allowed us to dive into PwC's innovation world and go beyond and above the kind of growth and incubation we expected," says Uptime's cofounder and CEO Augustin Celier. "They coached us and we learned a lot from being introduced to their partners. They bring a lot in terms of advice and sharing their expertise."

A second company that worked within PwC's programs is Zenbase, whose pioneering product is a chatbot that collects HR feedback. Zenbase reaches out every week on platforms like Messenger and Slack and asks a few simple questions that can be both qualitative and quantitative to assess everything from progress on specific projects to feelings of connectedness and morale. Managers can then access these data and respond accordingly. Via the PwC incubation program, Zenbase has been able to draw on data scientists, IP lawyers and cybersecurity experts, and may even be able to work with PwC as its debut client. "Joining DIVN is a great opportunity," says Robin Jeannel de Thiersant, Zenbase's cofounder and CEO. "PwC is very well connected and is going to help us sell our solution to the companies they know, B2B mode. PwC gives us access to key resources for the project; we especially valued being put in touch with data scientists and UX designers."

[Contact]   Smart-up solutions: **marc.ghiliotti@fr.pwc.com**
            Accelerator program: **philippe.kubisa@fr.pwc.com**
            Incubator program: **david.cohen-boulakia@fr.pwc.com**

[Links]   Web: **divn.fr** / **pwcaccelerator.com** / **pwc.fr/smart-up** Twitter: **@PwC_France**

"We strive to put our firm's expertise and network at the disposal of entrepreneurs to support, accelerate and derisk their journey towards achieving success."

Maria Luisa Silva, Marc Genevois, Sébastien Gibier / SAP (Startup Focus)

Global Director Market Enablement and GTM, SAP Startup Focus / Managing Director, SAP France / Head of Startups, SAP France

The Startup Focus program is SAP's global accelerator. It works with technology startups that target the global enterprise customer. The program is designed to enable young companies in big data, machine learning, artificial intelligence, IoT, and predictive and real-time analytics spaces to develop new applications using SAP technology and later contribute to accelerate their market traction. Founded in 2012, this virtual accelerator initiative serves as SAP's primary tool for connecting with the global startup community and building an open innovation ecosystem. The program has worked with over 5,500 startups to date, providing its members access to SAP technology, as well as technical expert guidance, marketing and sales enablement support and up to US$25,000 worth of credits and certifications.

"Our program is very broad," says Maria Luisa Silva, global director GTM, Startup Focus program at SAP (directly responsible for EMEA), calling from Luxembourg. "We effectively target technology startups that develop solutions that can unveil the potential our technology can provide. The startups' solutions in our portfolio focus in diverse industries, from manufacturing and healthcare to fintech and retail – most support or accelerate the reality of intelligent businesses in a smart world enabling smart lives. Ultimately, SAP's ambition is to help the world run better and improve people's lives. Startups are a part of this vision." Once startups have completed development, they initiate GTM phase, where they have the potential to access SAP's global customer base to showcase and sell their solutions. To date, over 260 fully validated solutions have emerged from the program.

The program is sponsored by SAP's managing director for France, Marc Genevois, whose stated ambition is to be "the innovation enabler for our customers, including startups." Marc has hired Sébastien Gibier to nurture and support the local startup ecosystem, which includes taking part in high-profile events such as VivaTechnology Paris and Le Grand Prix de l'Innovation de la Mairie de Paris.

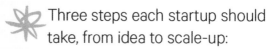 Three steps each startup should take, from idea to scale-up:

- Partner with a strong technology company that can provide you tools and support during the scaleup process.

- Invest in getting flagship customers' references.

- Align with market-relevant service-delivery partners in the geographies you want to grow in.

Dos & Don'ts:

Do be creative and original, but validate with your target market before jumping in.

Do think ahead and have a clear view of your goals.

Do have a definite vision of the market and don't try to move too fast.

Don't stay alone – network, create partnerships, share your ideas.

Don't overestimate your solution. The market is hyperdynamic; you should be too.

Don't spread yourself too thin by trying to do everything at once. Focus and excel.

"I would say we have a very dynamic ecosystem in France now," explains Marc. "A few years ago, corporates were attempting to acculturate to the startup way of working without doing real business. Now we have very mature corporates, many of whom have open innovation departments. The three key areas we are currently focusing on are the industry of the future, where we try to find and embrace new startups in the French ecosystem; HR, which is a very dynamic sector in Paris, with over 150 startups currently; and retail and e-commerce, where a lot of changes are requested by customers. There are other interesting aspects of the French ecosystem too, of course – for example, we have a strong ecosystem of engineering schools, which means programmers and developers are much cheaper here than in Silicon Valley, and that makes lower-cost development possible here." SAP France organizes many meetups, like SAP Tech me up, SAP Build the Next (industry/LoB focused) and SAP Startup Friday Pitch.

Case Studies

Headquartered in Paris, Meteo Protect offers solutions that measure the potentially adverse impact of weather conditions on businesses. Their solutions allow companies to cover against increased costs, offset declines in turnover and limit the volatility of financial results from one year to the next. Since joining the SAP program in 2014, the company has grown to become the insurance and reinsurance broker with the largest team in Europe dedicated exclusively to weather risk management, opened offices in London and Mumbai, entered a strategic partnership with banking group BNP Paribas and has been showered with awards. "Beyond the huge technology advantage that we gained through access to the SAP HANA in-memory platform, which for a startup was a game-changer in itself, the amazing support in sales and marketing as well as education and mentoring we received from SAP's Startup Focus Program has been a key driver of Meteo Protect's growth," says Meteo Protect's Gabriel Gross, president and founder.

Indigo Media onboarded with Startup Focus in April 2016. The company's IoT-solution allows retailers, brands and spaces to transform and drive their customers' experience in a completely personalized and interactive way, bringing the concept of "machine–human" interaction to a completely new level. In practice, the solution means that retailers will have access to deep analysis of their product performance and will be able to better control their campaigns in real-time. "One of the biggest added values for us of using SAP was the ability to deploy our solution on a proven and robust technology that can rapidly scaleup from a POC to an industrial solution," says Guillaume Walline, cofounder and CEO of Indigo Media. "Furthermore, being part of the StartUp Focus Group gave us the opportunity to reach new partners, clients and prospects."

[Contact]   Email: **luisa.silva@sap.com** / **sebastien.gibier@sap.com**

[Links]   Web: **startups.sap.com** Twitter: **@SAPStartups** / **@SAPFrance**

"We are building an open innovation ecosystem based on the creation of value-driven software offerings by our startup members. These address our customers' challenges and accelerate their journey towards winning in the digital economy."

Eric Texier
/ Sodexo

Group VP, Innovation

"Technology is rapidly evolving and opening up new ways of communicating. This creates new channels of interaction and transaction for consumers," says Eric Texier, Sodexo's group VP, innovation. "In addition, customers demand greater time optimization, convenience and personalization as their habits are changing. Evolving consumer expectations and disruptive technologies, in addition to the changing nature of services create a new competitive landscape. For Sodexo, this is an opportunity to provide new and better services and enhanced experiences to the people it serves."

Sodexo, founded in 1966, is a global leader in services that improve quality of life. The company provides integrated offerings – developed over fifty years of experience – that include food services, reception, safety, maintenance, cleaning and facilities and equipment management, employee rewards and benefits, in-home assistance, child care centers and concierge services. The company, which operates across eighty countries and serves seventy-five million consumers every day, has been working actively with external ecosystems through multiple strategic partnerships in open innovation in order to enhance existing services as well as develop the services of the future.

Since 2014, the group has partnered with the Crédit Agricole (CA) and global companies such as IBM, Sanofi, Phillips and Microsoft to create the Village by Crédit Agricole, a physical space in the heart of one of Paris's major business districts that's entirely devoted to business and innovation. In July 2015, Sodexo became a founding partner of thecamp, a European innovation campus set to open in the third quarter of 2017 that will allow interaction with startups, as well as public sector actors and private companies. And in 2016, Sodexo founded Sodexo Ventures, a venture capital fund that has already begun investing in startups with high growth potential in line with Sodexo's current or future activities.

Three steps each startup should take, from idea to scale-up:

- Dream big, but start small.

- Learn how to manage your growth, and start by learning how to be a manager.

- Align with a corporate partner who can open up new markets to your business.

Dos & Don'ts:

Do choose a mentor you can trust.

Do surround yourself with those who share your vision.

Do put people first.

Don't lose your agile mindset.

Don't be afraid of making mistakes.

Don't wait to think about going global.

In addition, Sodexo, with five other partners, created the Spark Life Contest, a pan-European startup challenge to bring the most innovative startups proposing solutions for tomorrow's quality of life. "We very much believe in fair, balanced and win-win relationships with startups," says Eric. "With over thirty-three thousand operational sites, Sodexo is able to provide startups with unparalleled opportunities in terms of capabilities and markets to test and deploy their innovations. The group operates in B2B environments corresponding to seven different segments and industries as well as pure B2C environments. The fact that our ecosystem spans eighty countries will help startups grow internationally at a rapid pace."

Case Studies

Sodexo's strategic partnership with the Village by CA allowed the group to meet Wynd, a French startup that was founded in 2013 and aims to connect the in-store (digital for store) and the out-of-store (web to store) worlds. Wynd offers a full solution to manage onsite and offsite sales, a unified back-office to handle operations and CRM, and a solution to authorize and process on-site and off-site payments. Together, Sodexo and Wynd have been working to reinvent the customer experience for Sodexo's consumers. Their collaboration has resulted in Click & Collect, an application designed to customize, streamline and enhance the customer journey at Sodexo's corporate sites and affiliated restaurants. Ismael Ould, CEO and cofounder of Wynd, says: "After building a rewarding partnership over the past year, we are delighted to continue to grow our business with Sodexo, with whom we share the same values and ambition to revolutionize the consumer experience."

To better address the increasing number of self-employed professionals and the arrival of the more "digitally native" Generation Y on the job market, Sodexo has invested in Neo-nomade, a platform developed by a Paris-based startup that enables professionals to find workplaces that are suitable to their personal requirements and locations. According to a survey conducted by Randstad in 2016, 64 percent of employees would like to work from home. Aware that much of today's global workforce is connecting to the cloud and not working from any fixed place, Sodexo had been looking at new technologies that favor mobility, sharing and the optimization of resources. With this investment, the company will have the opportunity to offer a range of services to office spaces covered by the Neo-nomade platform.

[Contact]   Mirella Marcon / Open Innovation Director
Tel: +33 6 08 36 08 91 Email: mirella.marcon@sodexo.com

 [Links]   Web: sodexo.com Twitter: @SodexoGroup

" *With over fifty years of experience under our belt, we can help startups win the race against time. You have to be lightning fast to seize all of the opportunities out there; and yet, it's all about the long haul.* "

Sofiane Ammar
/ thecamp

Partner

"thecamp aims to become the first European campus dedicated to emerging technology and social innovation. Its very concept is to look at how we can create the next steps of innovation within an ecosystem that could have several players – not only the classic mix of corporates and startups, but also representatives of cities, students and SMEs that can work together to build a more sustainable world," explains Sofiane Ammar, cofounder and managing director of thecamp's accelerator. thecamp is being built on a seventeen-acre site close to the scenic Sainte-Victoire mountain ridge in Aix-en-Provence. Inspired by traditional American campuses, its ambition is to be an ecosystem of connected intelligence, creation and innovation by focusing on seven main activities: a post-graduate training center, programs to prepare managers and executives in the private and public sectors, youth camps, an accelerator for startups and growing SMBs (supported by international mentors and entrepreneurs in residence teams), an experimentation center for cities, conferences open to the public and general interest challenges.

"One of the strongest assets of the acceleration program is connecting our global corporate partners to our selected startups in order to build strong business relationships," says Sofiane. "We have two main focuses. One is the mentoring program structured with international mentors, successful entrepreneurs and soft-skills mentors, partly here on the campus and partly remote. The second is the intrapreneurship aspect, which consists of cocreating startups with executives, managers and employees from corporates. We provide them with teams of coders, designers and collective-intelligence thinkers. As employees of thecamp's cofounding partners, such as Sodexo or AccorHotels, they will make their own brilliant minds available to work with our teams to codevelop and cocreate sustainable solutions. The Cisco Spin In program is our model here. In terms of applications, we mostly work B2B or B2B2C. It's very open in terms of topics, but of course anything connected with sustainability and smart cities is especially relevant, which can mean anything from food and education to banking and social projects."

Three steps each startup should take, from idea to scale-up:

- Plan your financing from the beginning to understand your sales cycle.

- Scale your local business and target a critical mass of revenue before building subsidiaries.

- Target margin rather than revenue to scale up the business in B2B and B2B2C activities.

Dos & Don'ts:

Do set up priorities and focus on them, whatever happens during your day.

Do read news related to your field – at least thirty minutes per day.

Do monitor your product's market fit through your leads and customers to stay on top of your company's financing.

Don't manage without empathy – show you have the right energy and passion to engage your team.

Don't hesitate to reset priorities if you don't see any customer success.

Don't scale up your global team without having a strong core team with clear responsibilities.

The campus will host up to forty startups each year, eventually cocreating with more than twenty-five intrapreneurs over a five-year period – startups that will stay at thecamp for an average of six months. The total budget for thecamp is eighteen million euros provided by heavy-hitter founders including Cisco, Crédit Agricole (Village by CA), Accenture and major local French public institutions. The key difference, says Sofiane, between thecamp and other startup campuses is the unique mix of private and public commitment. "Our job is to push and transform the mindset of our stakeholders in both spheres in order to remain more holistic and inclusive. It's not just about technology or use cases, but also about social-minded thinking, about how we can define the next style of philanthropy, or create the next social project for smart cities. The world is still largely driven by the idea of what societies can create for businesses, but thecamp is set up to challenge this mentality. Even our lab is a much more public arena where companies can verify their projects via two or three million citizens rather than a usual prototype lab. We want to not only live, create, work and study all in the same place but also transform mindsets to fully create and engage with a newly sustainable world."

Case Studies

"The idea for the Spark Life Initiative actually came via Sodexo, which has a big conference every two years around the theme of quality of life," explains Sofiane. "We at thecamp and several of our corporate sponsors decided to form a European contest that could help us select the best startups that could deliver the best or most ambitious project around this theme." The event begins in Paris before moving around Europe. "It's a bit different from a classic contest where you get money," says Sofiane. "With Spark Life it's about connecting innovations to existing products or themes and potentially executing proof of concept with the right partner; we are convinced that six months working with an international corporate has more value than cash. Although we are coordinators and facilitators of the Spark Life Initiative, along the way we are of course also looking for startups we can work with at thecamp's own accelerator and incubator."

[Contact]   Email: **sofiane@thecamp.fr** Tel: **+33 6 12 13 64 90**

[Links]   Web: **thecamp.fr** Facebook: **thecamp.provence** Twitter: **@thecampprovence**

"*The world is still largely driven by the idea of what societies can create for businesses, but thecamp is set up to challenge this mentality.*"

views

Frédéric Mazzella

CEO / BlaBlaCar

Before becoming a pioneer of people-powered travel networks, Frédéric Mazzella worked as a scientific researcher at NASA (USA) and NTT (Japan). He holds an MBA from INSEAD, a master's in computer science from Stanford, and a master's in physics from École Normale Supérieure (France). Frédéric is passionate about high social impact solutions, and is also an accomplished classical pianist.

Could you describe your entrepreneurial path and the moment you realized what you wanted to do?

The moment I realized that entrepreneurship was a viable path was when I was still living in California, at Stanford, finishing my master's in computer science. At the time, I was also working for NASA, and I was in a lab with really brilliant people. But I started noticing that a lot of them were dropping out of their studies and were, instead, launching or joining startups. You have to remember that this was in 1999 when Google was just starting, so it was new energy – powerful energy. Some of my friends left school for Google. I guess that's when I began looking at entrepreneurship as a real idea. I realized it was possible to leave your studies and to step away from a traditional path. I saw that really clever people were doing this, that it wasn't some kind of dropout story.

I continued working for NASA for a few years, and then I moved back to France where I worked for an American software company. In the company where I was working, I was not included or heard on some strategic decisions. I thought they really weren't in the best interests of the company, but I couldn't do anything about it. It was a real source of frustration because I was being forced to carry out a strategy I knew was not a winning one. I think this is where I began feeling a desire to change my path. In 2004, I began to resource all of my ideas. I must have had twenty different new company ideas, but the one that was really convincing was BlaBlaCar.

How did the idea of BlaBlaCar come about?

The story is perhaps well known now, but in 2003 I was working in Paris. I wanted to go home for Christmas to see my parents, who live about 500 km from the city, but I didn't have a car, and all the trains were full and really expensive for the holidays. But I knew I wasn't alone. I knew that Paris and other cities in France were full of people who didn't own cars and wanted to get somewhere. And likewise, I saw that there were many people leaving the city with space in their cars. This is when I began to envision a new travel network. I remember telling my parents about my idea when it was in the early stages, and I remember them saying, "We don't know if it will work or not, but at least we'll get to see you more."

And how did it work out?

From the beginning, I told myself, if this is going to work, it's going to work well. I knew it had the potential to be massive, and, as a carpooling platform, the only way it could substantially exist was as a big and ever-expanding market. And that's what it is – a marketplace. The more people use it, the more people need it. I always thought it would be what it is today, which is 40 percent of users between eighteen and thirty-five years old, with four out of ten people in France enrolled.

What were your early struggles and how did you overcome them? What mistakes did you make?

My initial idea for this long-distance platform – a peer-to-peer model – was that drivers could offer their seats to passengers going the same way. But early on, we got a lot of requests from companies who wanted to offer the service to their employees. The idea was to connect colleagues going from home to work and vice versa. At this point we weren't really making much revenue yet. We had users, but the company needed more time to grow into its model so, searching for stability, we decided to say "okay" to these companies. And that meant we spent a lot of time in the early days building platforms for these companies. I think we built over 200 platforms, one for each company.

" My best decision was articulating the values of the company. Doing this exercise, participating in the coconstruction of the atmosphere of BlaBlaCar, continues to be one of the highlights of our foundation and what invigorates our work and community. "

This was not scalable, as each client wanted a different tailored product. It slowed down our evolution. But I guess I wouldn't call it a mistake because it was a challenge, and it helped us with revenues. You have to remember that when we were founded, the sharing economy was in its infancy. It was 2006, so working on the B2B segment was a good way for the company to get funded until we could grow our C2C activity, but it was a time when our original product was put to the test in an interesting way.

What was your best decision?

My best decision was articulating the values of the company. Doing this exercise, participating in the coconstruction of the atmosphere of BlaBlaCar, continues to be one of the highlights of our foundation and what invigorates our work and community. We created a set of ten values together when we were a staff of only sixty people, and it's been the backbone for our expansion. I think it's the best thing you can do for your company, to bring everybody together and get on the same page. We have grown fast but, because of this early step, we have not broken our culture.

Could you describe your daily routine? How do you stay focused? What drives you?

Actually, I don't have that many routines, and perhaps I don't really like them. I'm a product guy. I have a routine in prioritizing and articulating the vision of what you're building. I organize my time around these centers. For the past eight or nine months, I've been working on BlaBlaLines, our new application for daily commute. But I'd have to say that I lived this creation – really focused on this product. But I guess, after that, I could say I work every day, morning to night. My day consists of meetings and discussions. I meet entrepreneurs every day; I'm very connected to the Paris ecosystem. In the end, what really defines our humanity is creativity and our social links, social interactions. This is what I believe.

What advice would you give to people in the early stages of starting up?

Make sure you know what you want and say no to the wrong opportunities. You're flooded by wrong opportunities. You have to decide which cards to discard, which ones to keep.

How do you maintain a work–life balance?

That's a tough one. I'm getting better. Over the past three years, I've been paying more attention to that. I try to keep some time for myself, to stop work on mobile devices on the weekends, but it's a struggle. I'm still not very good at it.

What do you like about having a startup in Paris?

Having a startup in Paris is the best of both worlds. You've got the excitement of the high-tech environment and companies, you've got the people you work with who are very passionate about new technologies, and then you've got Paris, with its diversity, its quality of life. I love living here because you can meet all kinds of people. If I compare it with Silicon Valley, Paris is so much richer. Silicon Valley is the molding factory of startups. You will always meet these people. But here in Paris, you have lots of artists, people that work in different industries. This is very refreshing. There's a very lively and active social scene here.

[About]   BlaBlacar is the largest carpooling platform in the world. Members register and create an online profile, which includes a "BlaBla measurement" – ratings and reviews by other members, social network verification and rate of response.

[Links]   Web: **blablacar.com** Facebook: **BlaBlaCar** Twitter: **@BlaBlaCar** Instagram: **BlaBlaCarFR**

What are you reading?
TechCrunch.

What are you listening to?
Various styles of music, from Chopin to
Karsh Kale, U2 to Norah Jones.

What's your favorite app?
Easy: BlaBlaCar.

What skill do you wish you had?
The power to know the truth immediately.

Marie Ekeland

Cofounder / daphni

Marie Ekeland is cofounder of daphni. She is also cofounder and vice-president of France Digitale, an association of founders and investors created to develop the French digital ecosystem. Marie serves as a board member for Parrot and Showroomprivé, and is a member of the French Digital Council and of the Startup Europe Advisory Board. She began her career in 1997 at JPMorgan in New York as a computer scientist. In 2000, Marie joined CPR Private Equity as a venture capitalist. She moved to Elaia Partners in 2005, and lead investments in Criteo, Edoki Academy, mobirider, Pandacraft, Scoop.it, Teads, Wyplay and Ykone, among others.

What led you towards the startup world?

Before becoming a founder, I was an engineer. At Université Paris-Dauphine, I majored in computer science, and my first job after this degree was in coding. I worked for JPMorgan in the late 90s, but I didn't feel satisfied, and I eventually decided that coding for trading floors was not for me.

I went back to school in 2000 to study economics at École d'économie de Paris. At some point, I crossed paths with Xavier Lazarus, who talked to me about startups and the rich ecosystem alive and prospering in Paris. He was starting the venture capital activity of Banque CPR, a French bank, and asked me to join. I felt my tech profile made sense there. It gave me a kind of purpose, to think of giving entrepreneurs a chance to live their dreams, to realize their goals.

How did you become a founder?

In the past seventeen years, I have been moving more and more towards an entrepreneurial path. In 2014, I left Elaia, and I knew I wanted to start something else. Two things happened while I was at Elaia. First, I grew more confident in my vision and in the power of the community through the cofounding of France Digitale. I began to see what I wanted my next project to be. I was searching for something that corresponded with my vision.

Second, I had the chance to seed a company, Criteo, which is one of the biggest tech companies in the French ecosystem and was one of its first international successes. What I witnessed as a board member showed me what it means to scale at the international level. All of this led me to have the faith to cofound daphni with four others so that we could create a community-based venture fund and create more value at scale.

So, why daphni?

I believed in what was happening in Paris and in Europe, but saw that no entrepreneur had enough of a critical mass in its local market in Europe to build a digital leader without going abroad very quickly. I wanted to help startups optimize their potential, to help promote international leaders who could benefit from the network effects of the digital economy.

Venture is about craftsmanship, so the question is how can you make it scale. In France, we were dealing with a few obstacles. People were seeing tech as just a sector and not a transformative power. Even though we saw the revolution in music and communication, we were not yet realizing how it was changing everything. It drove me and my cofounders to the conclusion that venture was going to be disrupted by digital and that we could use the new startup "rules" to make it more scalable, to help our companies on the international front. daphni was founded with this in mind; our number one value is to help our startups grow internationally, to have macro vision. We wanted to build a new model, relying on a community and a digital platform that connected geographically dispersed experts in diverse fields to build a collaborative and inquisitive network.

What did you expect to happen? What do you feel about what has happened?

What I remember being surprised by was the support we as the founding team received as an entrepreneurial team. daphni is built around a community model, and we had to build that community first. We reached out first to entrepreneurs, and the energy that they gave us and the enthusiasm that they showed were actually what held us up through the first growing pains. We worked hard to define the European DNA, which is at the core of our investment strategy: collectiveness, quality of life and inventiveness. We were also focused on being more open, more helpful, and this attitude really brought people together. Our early community was so enthusiastic, and so our daphni ambition actually grew with that.

"*I was very open with all of my contacts, so I got real, honest feedback and thus real interest. I would say you must approach people that are different from you and not only from the same industry.*"

What were your early struggles? How did you overcome them?

One thing that was complicated for me was finding the founding team, finding people with whom I shared the right DNA – same ambition, same wish for risks. If I hadn't found Willy Braun, Mathieu Daix, Pierre-Eric Leibovici and Pierre-Yves Meerschman, I wouldn't have been able to do this. When I left Elaia, I left alone, knowing that I would have to find my own way.

But in fact, my cofounders were there all along, I knew each of them as previous co-investors or from working together at France Digitale, but it took some time to come together as a team. Pierre-Eric, Pierre-Yve, and I have VC backgrounds, and Willy and Mathieu bring the "*savoir faire*" in community building. All five of us understood the weaknesses of the current VC models, shared the same vision and values. We think of ourselves as this evolution away from old models; this was really important in our founding. This is why we call ourselves mutant venture capitalists.

Once you identified your founding team, what was the essential next step?

Our model was articulated on a digital platform, but none of us had ever been a CTO in a previous life. Our community, which is very diverse in skill, understood that we needed an internal tech team from scratch. Our strategy was tech-centric, so, of course, we needed to develop this. At this point, we had to think more as a startup. We had to leave some of our old VC reflexes and really dig into a different mentality of creation. This was the essential next step for us and a really important moment in the solidification of daphni.

What professional advice would you give someone in the early stages of their startup?

Something that really helped me out was meeting with a lot of people and getting their opinions. I was very open with all of my contacts, so I got real, honest feedback and thus real interest. You must approach people that are different from you and not only from the same industry. I didn't only talk to other VCs. I traveled, too, to San Francisco, London, Berlin, New York in an effort to understand new models in VCs and get benchmarks at the international level. I talked to entrepreneurs to see how venture could evolve from their perspective, and I reached out to and spent a lot of time discussing with academics. I was trying to get insight from as many different worlds as possible. This is essential in the beginning. These conversations really opened my eyes and gave me more angles with which to approach my future projects. Seeking out other people builds a complete image, and it expands your expertise and also your geographic network.

Could you describe your daily routine? What drives you?

It is very important for me to maintain a balance between my rhythm of work, leisure and travel, between being in the middle of it all, being with my family and friends and being alone. I work very long hours but I take frequent holidays with my husband and children, and like interacting from time to time with their school environment and friends. I establish time for myself wherein I won't be interrupted and wherein I can digest everything. I need these alone moments, and most of the time these happen when I travel. I associate reflection with travel.

What do you recognize as your strengths and weaknesses?

The thing I'm really bad at is answering all my emails. If I see that the response takes more than a second, I know I want to really reflect and give it time. But inevitably emails continue to come in, in droves, and it's hard for me to keep up with all of them. On the other hand, I do not lose focus on my priorities and manage to make them move forward without being drowned by external solicitation.

What do you like about the Paris ecosystem?

I find a lot of diverse products and companies in Paris: startups are addressing important challenges like agriculture, healthcare, environmental, education issues and are not afraid of industrial or scientific challenges. What will lead to continued growth and success for Parisian startups is if they build companies that have personal meaning and are not afraid of tech complexity. They are not simply saying, I want to change the world; they're saying, I want to change the world for the better. For example, daphni's first investment was in Agricool, a startup founded by two sons of farmers who are transforming containers to grow tasty and healthy fruits and vegetables in cities at scale. I also like that entrepreneurs, like Agricool's founders, are younger. To me, that means it's a viable path after studies, that more and more students are aspiring to entrepreneurship, and that it will, in turn, sustain and establish the right level of energy and disruption in the ecosystem.

[About]   daphni is an international venture capital mutant that is committed to evolving methodologies and community-building within the startup ecosystem of Europe and beyond. Using a digital platform, daphni connects startups with diverse thought-leaders, investors and groundbreaking services to advance civic and creative endeavors that will improve the world.

[Links]   Web: daphni.com Facebook: daphnipolis Twitter: @daphnipolis

What are you reading?
Sostiene Pereira by Antonio Tabucchi, very relevant in the
current political climate; Veronique Ovaldé's novels – I love
her female characters; and the series *Le poids des secrets*
by Aki Shimazaki – the same story told by five different
characters, an enlightening experience.

What's your favorite app?
Keakr. And Lunchr. Two mutant startups.

What's your favorite podcast?
Freakonomics.

What are your work essentials?
Two of daphni's core values: "style matters" and
"question, listen, act."

What skill do you wish you had?
Understanding people's inner drives at first sight.

Quentin Sannié

Cofounder and CEO / Devialet

Impressed by his uncle's creative path, Quentin Sannié felt he had an entrepreneurial spirit from a very early age. Upon his admittance to Université Paris-Dauphine, Quentin found himself wanting to live more than just a student's life. Realizing early on the impact computers would have on the future of business, Quentin bought his first Apple and began training local Paris business owners. Today, still on the cutting edge of technology, Quentin is the cofounder and CEO of Devialet, the international leader in high-end amplifiers and sound engineering.

How would you describe your path towards entrepreneurship?
I went to Université Paris-Dauphine, where I studied management and economic science and eventually received my master's in technology management and strategy. Throughout my last two years in this program, I launched my first company. It was 1985, and Apple had just released its first Macintosh. I remember the day I bought mine. I had run to the bank to ask for a loan so that I could buy one. It was a very emotional day for me. I already knew that this thing I was going to bring home with me would change everything. I set up my first company, helping introduce people to these new Mac tools. I worked with architects, doctors; I assisted small companies as they integrated this technology into their business.

In fact, I was never happy just being still; I wasn't happy just being a student. I felt I wasn't active enough. I thought that I needed to do more, be more efficient. And I wanted to be earning money. That's why the release of the Mac gave me some purpose. Today, when I look back at this time period, I think I was completely crazy. When I see my children now, they have no complex like this, but, honestly, I loved this period. It was very exciting, and the mood at Dauphine was very pro-active, very encouraging.

Did you always identify as an entrepreneur?

Well, yes, I imagine. It started when I was very young, when I was maybe ten or eleven years old. I remember my uncle, [cofounder] Emmanuel Nardin's father, was an architect, and his way of life and creation was very inspirational to me. I like that he was always looking towards the new, towards a problem and a solution to it. He told us, "What is really important in life is what you are able to create. In the end, that is the most important thing you can do." These words really stayed with me, and I still think that what I'm able to create is the meaning of life, the meaning of my life. I have four children. I have set up many companies in my life. It was really the goal of my life from the very beginning, to build something. I didn't want to be managed by others. I wanted to invent my own life, I wanted to do new things every day. I wanted to achieve something, and I knew that meant that I would have to be the leader of something. I don't consider myself superior to others. But I do think life is short, so I will make the most of my time here. Time goes by very quickly.

And how does it feel to be an entrepreneur in France?

In France, things have completely changed in the past five to seven years. Now being an entrepreneur is very trendy. It's considered positive. It's considered helpful for the society, for the nation. But this feeling is rather new. The French tech movement helped us a lot to change this reputation. Now I'm considered someone who is really useful and influential for the country. But it's a new sense.

Still, I think France is a great place to begin a business. Globally, social laws protect the people, so it's more comfortable for everyone, for businesses and their employees. In Paris, our engineers are some of the best, really skilled, so, as a tech company, it's wonderful to be in this country. Beyond that, though, it's never easy to be an entrepreneur. It's never easy to try to make something different. Obviously, the market is huge in the US, but it varies state to state. I consider myself lucky to be in this country, at this time, in Paris.

" *Don't be afraid of being really, really ambitious, but don't be ambitious for yourself. Be ambitious for your project.* "

How would you describe your struggles as an entrepreneur?

If you are climbing Mount Everest, you might be freezing, but you know it's been your choice to freeze. In a sense, you are able to cherish the hardship on the way to the reward. Personally, I love competition. At Devialet, we love competition when it is difficult because it means we are going somewhere new, that we are a part of change and innovation. Certainly, we also know that we can fail. It's just that we are not scared of that. We accept that it's a likelihood, an inevitability.

I have failed many times. In 2008, during the financial crisis, I had a consulting firm specializing in strategy and acceleration of growth, new business models. Business became difficult, so I decided to shut down this company at the end of that year. We stopped our studies, investment stopped. And I remember the day I closed the company. It was a rainy morning in December, you know, one of those sad Paris winter days. I remember walking out of the doors of the Tribunal de Commerce and feeling, in fact, very happy. Despite the weather, despite it being the end, I was proud of myself, I felt strong to have admitted that it was over. You don't know where you are going after that, but it's almost inspiring. I walked home that day, in that rain, that grey; it was very intense. It was time to restart, and what I didn't know exactly then was that this would be the very beginning of Devialet.

How do you maintain a work–life balance?

Every day I'm home by 8:30 PM, and every day I start work at 8:30 AM. My schedule is, in essence, quite regular, but I have to have my work day. It gives me a sense of self. I have four sons, and my wife is good about reminding me to sign out of work. She is very supportive, and she knows how important my entrepreneurial life is. She is a stability for us all. You know, when you are an entrepreneur, your partner is incredibly important. It would have been absolutely impossible to achieve what we have without my wife, even if she's not in the business. She encourages me, and she's understanding of the trials and tribulations of the very hard periods. It's a kind of proof of love when someone is able to support you when life is very complicated.

What advice would you give to young entrepreneurs?

Even if it's cliché, I must say that you have to believe in yourself, in your ability. Don't be afraid of being really, really ambitious, but don't be ambitious for yourself. Be ambitious for your project. Even if it's opening a restaurant, make it your best. Search out every idea for design, location, hiring and concept. It's going to be hard, but it's more exciting when you try to achieve something, to be unique. What is good about mediocrity? Why do it if you don't want it to be special?

On top of that, my advice would be find your team. Your partners should be very different from you. Three me's is just three times the same, bland. You have to choose people with different skills from yours. Very often people create partnerships with people who are too similar to them in work ethic, in talent, in vision, and very often they don't push each other enough, preventing success.

[About] Founded in 2007 at the height of the startup wave in Paris, Devialet is one of the most successful entrepreneurship ventures in France. Devialet delivers cutting edge technologies in amplifiers and speakers. Created by engineer Pierre-Emmanuel Calmel, entrepreneur Quentin Sannié, and designer Emmanuel Nardin, Devialet lives in the heart of Paris and collaborates with a team of forty acoustic, mechanic and electrical engineers to build the future of sound.

[Links] Web: **devialet.com** Facebook: **quentin.sannie** Twitter: **@QuentinSannie**

What are you listening to?
I listen to a lot of music during the weekend. It could be Dire Straights, Mozart or Joan Baez.

What's your favorite app?
I use so many apps: Booking.com to quickly find a place to sleep while I'm in an Uber from the airport in whatever city I'm visiting.

What are your work essentials?
My brain, my team, my iPhone, my dreams for the future.

What skill do you wish you had?
To be a great pianist.

What time do you wake up in the morning?
It depends where I am on the planet. 7 AM in Paris; too early when I am jet-lagged in San Francisco or Seoul.

Stanislas Niox-Chateau

CEO and Founder / Doctolib

Before immersing himself in the world of startups, Stanislas Niox-Chateau was a top-level tennis player. Though an injury changed his life, it did not slow him down. While attending HEC in Paris, Stanislas became involved in several entrepreneurial businesses, including Balinea, while he worked towards the completion of his master's in finance, strategy and entrepreneurship. In 2013, after launching several booking platforms (Weekendesk and La Fourchette), Stanislas initiated Doctolib, a company now serving over 20,000 doctors in France and Germany and used by 8.2 million patients each month.

What did you do before becoming a founder?
As a child, my whole life was athletics. I was a professional tennis player, which means I traveled a lot, living for periods of time in Spain and in the US. After an injury, I had to give up my sports career. I was just seventeen, and I directed myself towards school and ended up attending HEC in Paris. I had a great community there, and in that environment I decided to launch my first company, Balinea, in 2010. I realized that the shift from sports to entrepreneurship made a lot of sense to me. I think athletes are like entrepreneurs; they work to perfect a product, which is their body, their performance or their game and then they tour that product in a competitive environment, challenging rivals and relating to an audience as much as possible.

Wishing to be closely involved in more entrepreneurial adventures, I cofounded Otium Capital, a French startup studio that specialized in online booking businesses. With my network we invested thirty-five million euro to launch online booking platforms such as Balinea (hairdressers, beauty salons and spas), Weekendesk (short break travels) and eventually La Fourchette (restaurants), which we later sold to TripAdvisor. Those were amazing experiences, but I wanted to start a project with greater value for a larger population. That's when I decided to launch Doctolib.

How did this idea come about?

I think the idea was rather obvious after all we had discovered in our earlier creations and investments related to booking. We simply found there was a serious need to find and easily make appointments with doctors and there was no existing technological solution to solve that problem efficiently. We started Doctolib with two main goals. First, we wanted to transform the healthcare industry, to improve access to doctors and hospitalization, by providing the best daily tool for all players. Second, we wanted to build a multi-thousand employee company with shared values and a rich culture. This culture would have to be at the very core of our DNA in order to allow us to grow and change the game quickly. Today this culture is symbolized by an acronym which is also our motto: the SPAAH – Service, Passion, Ambition, Attack (as in sports strategy) and Humility.

Developing the services Doctolib offers was also important on a more personal level, because I've had a stammer since I was young, and I remember how challenging it was for my parents to organize all of my medical visits. On top of that, as an athlete, I deepened my relationship with the medical industry. After my tennis injury, I needed a lot of complex treatment and care. When I started to be involved with online booking businesses, I knew healthcare would be the sector that would benefit the most from booking and that it would be my final destination.

And how is the business going? Did everything go to plan?

To be honest, we imagined this because our idea was simple, our goal was feasible – a website, an application connecting patients and doctors, facilitating a very common need. And it worked and is working. It connects people that need to connect and with a greater ease than previously existed. We spent a lot of time, and we were experienced enough to know how to make something that would suit our audience. Maybe the only thing we didn't forecast was the exponential growth we'd see. After three years, we are now at 320 employees, serving 8.2 million French and German patients, with 20,000 doctors on the platform every month. Basically, it's far beyond what we might have imagined. We've exceeded our own expectations.

" *When I think about who we are working for, in a sense, doctors and patients, I know I can't settle. It's easy for me to keep up my pace when I have this thought centered in my head.* "

What mistakes would you say you've made?

Well, we've made a lot, and we continue to make them. However, we usually find a good way to recover, and I hope that will continue, given we've spent a lot of time building a special team and developing our mission. The most difficult part was and remains hiring the right team members, especially when you must hire 200 people in two years. It's hard to find the right people. It's the most important challenge, but one we still enjoy.

And what has been your best decision?

Likewise, establishing a great team, finding my first ten people. My two cofounders. Yes, the first ten members of the team are my best choices.

What would you have done differently?

To be honest, I don't think like that at all. I think day-by-day. I truthfully cannot go to this place where you try to edit or relive your life having made other decisions. What is nice this time around, not as a professional tennis player but as someone in the startup ecosystem, is that I can run this marathon with a team. It's really step-by-step, each person for each person, but also step-by-step all together. For me, we have a long-term vision at Doctolib, so we really don't have time to stop running. But we're not trying to do it as a sprint. We are a true sports team – some people are on the field, some people are not on the field, some are coaches, managers, but we all want to achieve the same goal.

Could you describe your daily routine?

I have a very organized work style. I work 70–80 hours per week, and I really organize this time, hour after hour – 20 percent meetings, 20 percent independently working, 60 percent with my team, in the field or in workshops. I have a personal dashboard that is my go-to, my real compass. Doctolib also has an internal monitoring platform that is essential for how we all stay united in task and mission. When I think about who we are working for, in a sense, doctors and patients, I know I can't settle.

What do you like about running a startup in Paris?

Well, in truth, we have headquarters in Paris and Berlin. We have thirty-five offices, total, in both countries, but we're still 80 percent based in Paris. Without a doubt, France is the best country to launch a startup today, and I really believe what I'm saying. We have a lot of governmental help and an incredibly supportive ecosystem of programs and incubators, not to mention engaged investors. Plus, Paris, in particular, has a lot of talent, a lot of engineers, and a growing entrepreneurial mindset that is being recognized internationally. Obviously, expanding your startup becomes more complex in stages two and three, but for a beginning startup, I think Paris is an extraordinary environment.

What French startups inspire you?

Well, I am a fan of BlaBlaCar; they are friends and investors of Doctolib. But what really excites me about them is their vision, their international vision: in the past three years, they have successfully exported a service which is very popular in France in almost twenty countries. After that, I really like La Fourchette because I spent some time working on this project and I'm close to their CEO. Even with their rapid growth, they have maintained their original values and that's something we try to replicate at Doctolib.

What professional advice would you give someone in the early stages of their startup?

Know that it's only you and your cofounders who can make the best decisions for your business; do not delegate the hiring process to another organization. Also, put together your organization early, not only with hiring but with putting in place good practice, processes and tools that work and complement each other. And it's extremely important to see your customer directly in the field. You have to go to them, invite yourself. Really just speaking to your potential audience will improve your product enormously. I can't emphasize it enough – you really must think about your customer. Fundraising and strategy will sort itself out; you will find the right way if your product is right.

[About]   Doctolib is a web and mobile application that facilitates medical booking between patients and doctors. With just a few clicks, patients can see the availabilities of their doctors, and doctors can easily optimize their care and services. Doctolib currently serves over 20,000 doctors in France and Germany and is used by 8.2 million patients each month.

[Links]   Web: **doctolib.fr** Facebook: **stanislas.nioxchateau** Twitter: **@stanniox**

What are you reading?
The Alliance by Reid Hoffman and *Delivering Happiness*
by Tony Hsieh

What are you listening to?
Hans Zimmer. Great for focus and reminding yourself that
you're on an epic mission to change the world for the better.

What's your favorite app?
The Doctolib app, of course! Besides that I use the
G-suite apps to do the vast majority of my work.

What's your favorite podcast?
I mostly tune in to French radio, so it would have to be
l'After Foot by RMC, but when I have more time I enjoy
listening to the Harvard Business Review Ideacast.

What skill do you wish you had?
I wish I could speak all languages in the world
because communication is key.

191

Paulin Dementhon

Founder and CEO / Drivy

After graduating from HEC in 2002, Paulin Dementhon wanted to see the world. To achieve this, he embarked on a career in container shipping, which allowed him to live in both Hong Kong and São Paulo. After a few years, however, Paulin grew weary of this work and decided to revisit his desire to create his own company, launching a dynamic carpooling service called Quivaou.com in 2008. This project would eventually inspire him to develop Voiturelib in June 2010. After three years of growing success across France, however, Voiturelib, under Paulin's leadership, was looking towards international markets. In 2013, Voiturelib announced its ambition to touch lives in other European countries, changing its name to Drivy.

Where are you from and what did you do before?

I grew up in the suburbs of Paris, one of three children. Really nothing exceptional. When I graduated from business school at HEC in 2002, all I knew was that I wanted to travel, to explore the world and to do something a bit different from what most of my classmates that were heading into finance and marketing careers were doing. The first job I found that allowed me to do that was with a container shipping company based in Marseille. I worked for them for six years, and I really did travel and see parts of the world otherwise unknown to me. I was sent to Hong Kong and São Paulo. And this was really interesting, in its own way, to be a part of a big operational company, absolutely low-tech. It was not at all related to the startup world. I wasn't in that mindset yet, even if I always had ideas for new companies. I do think I've always had an entrepreneurial spirit.

And how did you become a founder?

When I turned thirty, I had one of those crisis moments, when I told myself, if I don't start something now, if I don't point myself in the direction I want to live, this life will never develop, will never be. Now, I know that the seed of Drivy was planted in me the first time I saw GPS phones coming onto the market. When I saw how people were using this gadget, I thought of one day creating a dynamic carpooling service. This was not really Drivy, yet, but it was the idea that motivated me to leave my job; it was the extremely risky and adventurous step I took to change my life. I really knew nothing about tech or the internet, but I learned. And here I am eight years later.

How did you learn? How did you begin?

Well, this was at the end of 2008. This is when my life changed, or rather, I changed my life. I started in Marseille, completely alone, without a network. I just started reading, watching videos, talking to people, organizing myself and ideas. I was learning about this world, about creating businesses, startups, about how to integrate and harness tech. However, the more I read, the more I tried, I began to realize that it would be very difficult to develop a tech company in Marseille. I don't know if I could have done it, but the startup culture, the image of the entrepreneur was not apparent in this city.

And now I realize that it really would have been impossible to start a tech platform for carpooling at that time; now it's clear to me that it wouldn't have worked. But I was still trying, I was always thinking about it. Then in early 2010, with the same mission in mind – to give freedom to people living in cities and to have a freedom that was community-based and sustainable – I saw there was another way to do it, to build a peer-to-peer car rental platform allowing car owners, if their cars stay parked 95 percent of the time, to put them on the platform, to trust in the platform with company insurance and customer service, etc., and to rent them to neighbors. I guess the start of Drivy was in the South, but I told myself I needed more of a network, so I moved myself to Paris, landed in the BlaBlaCar offices. I met the founder, Frédéric Mazella, because of my developing project, and they sublet me one table in their headquarters. I guess these were the humble beginnings.

" *I really believe in taking this time to define and picture how each person functions within the company to realize the vision of the company.* "

What was one of the best moments of this humble start?

One of the best moments happened during the first year, September 2010. I had put online a really simple, really crude version of the platform, and during this first month, I got a call from a user. I will never forget this day. He had called to complain. He was telling me all of the reasons why the platform was not good enough, that it needed a lot of improvement. Yet, his call showed me my audience. He had already done something like twenty rentals with this very basic thing I had put out there. I guess it was the day I realized how big this thing could be, how useful it really was. This guy wanted it to work for him. He was already a fan, in a sense. He just needed something that had fewer glitches.

And one of the worst moments?

Certainly one of the most complicated moments in our story was when we had to change our company name. We launched as Voiturelib, but, of course, it was confused with Autolib. And on top of that, it was in French. If we had any ambitions of expanding in Europe, internationally, it wouldn't go very far, you know. So, in 2013 we changed the company name. It was actually really painful. You don't realize what a name is until you're having to throw it away; you kind of lose part of yourself, your identity. It felt like a huge risk. You don't know what you'll lose, who you'll lose with a name change. We had our network in France who knew us as Voiturelib. We weren't sure where Drivy would take us. It was definitely a nervous time.

How would you describe your best decision?

One thing I did right was to spend a huge amount of time to really focus on product and user experience in the first few years. I refused a lot of partnerships and press opportunities because I wanted to be sure my product was good. I think you have to take that time to invest in the user's experience with your product. Otherwise, you risk a lot more in the way of failure. You risk completely losing your audience. I also spent a lot of time getting the organization right.

To know what functions you need and what job descriptions will look like is absolutely important. You need to benchmark with other companies, but also realize that each company is different, has different needs. Then, finding the right people that match and want to support this vision is irreplaceable. I really believe in taking this time to define and picture how each person functions within the company to realize the vision of the company.

How do you maintain a work–life balance?
When I started the company, I was a single man, running around, doing customer service on my cellphone. My work–life balance was pretty tough; it had no definition. I was giving everything to the company. Today, I still work pretty long hours, but it's more standardized. I stop at 8 PM. I take vacation and do my best to disconnect during the weekends. I enjoy my family. I cannot imagine a better job, so that makes me happy in my personal life. It's still intense and above average in quantity of work produced, but I do think I have found a way to balance. Recently, we really upgraded, added new positions. I went from having fifteen people reporting to me to seven. And that's changed everything. This structure I've created has given me my life back.

[About]   Drivy helps car owners maintain the care and usage of their car while connecting drivers-in-need with trustworthy vehicles. With the Drivy app, you can discover cars close to you that are available for rent. With partnerships across Europe, Drivy ensures that all parties are protected and ready for the road.

[Links]   Web: drivy.com Facebook: drivy.en Twitter: @drivy Instagram: drivyfr

What are you reading?
My two latest favorites have been *Freedom*
by Jonathan Franzen and *Sapiens: A Brief History
of Humankind* by Yuval Noah Harari.

What are you listening to?
French, Brazilian (after my time in São Paulo),
some international rock and classical music.

What are your work essentials?
A nice working space, full of light.

What skill do you wish you had?
I wish I could play music or sing.

What time do you wake up in the morning?
When my three-month-old daughter
wakes up. Around 7:30.

Guillaume Gibault

Founder & CEO / Le Slip Français

Guillaume Gibault founded Le Slip Français, a company that started off selling simple but chic men's underwear, in 2011. With a combination of business-school savvy, a good sense of humor and a creative approach to social media, he has managed to build a company that has maintained 100 percent per annum growth, runs three boutiques in Paris and has collaborated with the likes of Princesse tam.tam and American Vintage, among many other well-known brands. Today the company has diversified into boxers, swimsuits, socks and women's products, all of which are still manufactured entirely in France.

Where are you from and what did you study?
I am a true Parisian, born and raised, which is actually quite rare! I graduated from HEC business school in 2009, majoring in international commerce, which took me to NYC for six months and Milan for four months.

What was your entrepreneurial path, or the moment you realized what you wanted to do?
Like a lot of young people who graduated from business school, I wanted to start my own company, but I needed an idea – preferably one that felt new, that wasn't too money intensive and that could be successful using social media to grow the brand. I worked for two years at Bio c' Bio, an organic supermarket chain that was just starting at the time, and loved the experience. The company went from four to twelve shops in less than two years, and gave me the idea of starting my own thing.

How did the idea for your company come about?
Like a lot of people, I was looking for THE idea. I wanted to start in a field that I liked and that did not need that much money to start. Fashion sounded like a good idea, and thinking of internet and web sales, I figured that within fashion, underwear was most likely the best product to sell online because it's small, light, easy to ship and, most importantly, you don't try it on. Plus it's a big market with no cool brands for the past twenty years. Then I figured that Louis Vuitton and Hermes were great inspirations and their French savoir faire, *je ne sais quoi* and "Made in France" products were a tremendous asset to both starting a brand and building for the long term. Basically I was trying to come up with a cool, online Hermes-like underwear brand. That's how Le Slip Français was born.

At Le Slip Français, we are reinventing the way the whole fashion industry works and doing the exact opposite of what brands have been doing for the past thirty years. Our company not only shows the way things could work but also proves that it can actually be done. It's a great challenge, of course, but we work for a real cause: "You want to change the world? Start by changing your briefs!"

How important has social media been to your brand?
Social media has been key from the start for Le Slip Français. We started our Facebook page even before opening our website, and it's on Facebook that we have launched our most successful viral campaigns: La Surprise du Chef, Very Love Trip ... it's one of the channels that the brand is most known for, and a great way to interact daily with our community. In 2014, we launched our Instagram account and the community grew fast. We became one of the strongest French brands on the platform, and that attracted a lot of new members to our community and, eventually, new customers.

Do you have to travel much?
I travel a lot in France, meeting with our ten most important manufacturers, using France's greatest pride, the TGV (Train à Grande Vitesse, or "high-speed train"). All of them are within a three-hour train ride, and I actually wonder how other brands do it with suppliers across the world. I also travel once or twice a year abroad to our top four markets outside of France: the UK, Germany, the US and Japan. It's always very challenging as it feels like restarting the brand from zero each time, but it's also a great energy boost.

What keeps you excited, personally and professionally?
I like challenges. I like to learn new things, to build and experiment. My greatest fear is to regret not doing anything fun when I'm older, so I do my best to improve all the time. I constantly question the way I do things and try to come up with ideas that make a difference.

"*Figure out what you are best at and what makes you different from your competitors – and do only this.*"

When I started out, I was looking for adventure. I wanted to start a new kind of brand, manufacturing cool products in an authentic way and using social media to get awareness. I wanted to start something on my own, have fun and prove that the internet could help things work differently. It went way beyond my expectations .

What were some of the early obstacles you faced?

The hardest part for me was to convince the first textile factory to start producing for me. I was a young startup with no clients at the time, and I had to build trust and a true relationship to start the first production lines. Since then we have built the company on our strong ties with our twenty-seven suppliers, and we are really proud of it.

What was your best decision?

To focus on our key asset: online brand awareness through great content. Another of our big advantages was the Made in France element, which was a big part of our enterprise. It became a huge political slogan at the time, so we got lots of media attention for it, and now it's an industry-wide movement that's still growing.

I do wish we had joined Instagram earlier. A few American insta-brands, such as Daniel Wellington and Triangl swimwear, grew super fast from the start, and we caught up only two years later in 2014. Instagram is deeply transforming the fashion industry, and for a startup it's a great opportunity to get worldwide awareness using differentiating content that bigger companies are not agile enough to come up with. Video content, for example, is a tough challenge and a great way to generate interest.

What professional advice would you give to people in the early stages of starting up?

Figure out what you are best at and what makes you different from your competitors – and do only this.

What is your daily ritual?

Every morning I have a breakfast meeting at the very Parisian Café Le Moulin de la Vierge just in front of our office. I get in at around 9 AM and I never leave the office later than 8 PM. A good work–life balance is essential for me, and is one of the key reasons for starting my own business. I also box two to three times a week – it's how I get my best ideas.

What do you like about working in Paris?

I love everything about this city. It's been booming for the past five years with startups, restaurant, bars … everything is changing, and there is great energy in the air. I've built a strong network within the Paris startup ecosystem, and try to learn from everybody I meet. Understanding other companies' issues has always helped me come up with new ideas for our own company, and I love to be challenged on the way we do things, to keep improving. Life is about always learning new things!

[About]   Le Slip Français **is an underwear, swimwear and accessories brand, made entirely in France. With boutiques in France, Hong Kong, Japan, the UK, the US and many other countries, it also has a successful online shop.**

What are you reading?
La nuit sera calme by Romain Gary.

What are you listening to?
Juliette Armanet's "L'amour en Solitaire".

What's your favorite app?
City Mapper.

What are your work essentials?
My iPhone, MacBook air and a Parisian coffee.

What skill do you wish you had?
Writing.

What time do you wake up in the morning?
7:30. Okay, 8 AM

directory

Startups

Archive Valley
40 Quai de Jemmapes
75010 Paris
archivevalley.com

Baby Sittor
23 rue Blondel
75002 Paris
Babysittor.com

Compte-Nickel
18 avenue Winston Churchill
94220 Charenton-le-Pont
compte-nickel.fr

Dataiku
6 Boulevard Poissonnière
75009 Paris
dataiku.com

drust
43 rue du Faubourg
Saint-Antoine
75011 Paris
drust.io

Emiota
24 Impasse Mousset
75012 Paris
wearbelty.com

Innerspace VR
157 Boulevard MacDonald
75019 Paris
Innerspacevr.com

La Ruche qui dit Oui!
2 rue de la Roquette
75011 Paris
laruchequiditoui.fr

Never Eat Alone
19 rue Eugène Flachat
75017 Paris
nevereatalone.io

Stanley Robotics
96 bis Boulevard Raspail
75006 Paris
stanley-robotics.com

talent.io
13 rue d'Uzès
75002 Paris
talent.io

Ulule
8 rue Saint-Fiacre
75002 Paris
ulule.com

Programs

Agoranov
96 bis Boulevard Raspail
75006 Paris
agoranov.com

International au Féminin
intfem.com

Mission French Tech
Ministère de l'Economie
et des Finances
139 rue de Bercy
75012 Paris
frenchtechticket.com

NUMA Paris
39 rue du Caire
75002 Paris
paris.numa.co

Paris&Co
157 Boulevard Macdonald
75019 Paris
parisandco.com

Paris Pionnières
35 rue de Sentier
75002 Paris
pionnieres.paris.com

TheFamily
25 rue du Petit Musc
75004 Paris
thefamily.co

Spaces

Anticafé République
6 rue de Château d'Eau
75010 Paris
anticafe.eu

DRAFT Ateliers
12 Espl. Nathalie Sarraute
75018 Paris
Ateliers-draft.com

kwerk
44-46 rue de la Bienfaisance
75008 Paris
kwerk.fr

Le Laptop
6 rue Arthur Rozier
75019 Paris
lelaptop.com

Le Loft 50 Partners
62 rue Jean-Jacques
Rousseau
75001 Paris
50partners.fr

Liberté Living-Lab
9 Rue d'Alexandrie,
75002 Paris
liberte.paris

Nuage Café
14 rue des Carmes
75005 Paris
nuagecafe.fr

Partech Shaker
33 rue du Mail
75002 Paris
partechshaker.com

Station F
55 Boulevard Vincent-Auriol
75013 Paris
station.co

Experts

bluenov
96 Rue Edouard Vaillant
92300 Levallois-Perret, France
bluenove.com

JCDecaux
17 Rue Soyer
92200 Neuilly-sur-Seine
jcdecaux.com

Mission French Tech
Ministère de l'Economie
et des Finances
139 rue de Bercy
75012 Paris
lafrenchtech.com

OneRagtime
2 place d'Estienne d'Orves
75009 Paris
oneragtime.com

PwC
63 rue de Villiers
92208 Neuilly-sur-Seine Cedex
pwc.fr

SAP Startup Focus
35 rue d'Alsace
92300 Levallois-Perret
startups.sap.com

Sodexo
255 quai de la Bataille
de Stalingrad 92130
Issy-les-Moulineaux
sodexo.com

thecamp
245 Denis Papin
13100, Aix en Provence
thecamp.fr

Interviews

BlaBlaCar
6 rue Ménars
75002 Paris
blablacar.com

daphni
87 rue Réaumur
75002 Paris
daphni.com

Devialet
126 rue Réaumur
75002 Paris
devialet.com

Doctolib
32 rue de Monceau
75008 Paris
doctolib.fr

Drivy
35 rue Greneta
75002 Paris
drivy.com

Le Slip Francais
1 rue du Mail
75002 Paris
leslipfrancais.fr

Accountants

BDO Paris 07
Siège social
113 rue de l'Université
75007 Paris
bdo.fr

Elitax
19 quai de la Seine
75019 Paris
elitax.com

Exponens
20 rue Brunel
75017 Paris
exponens.com

Fi. Solutions
Siège Social
8 rue Bayen, 75017 Paris
fisolutions.fr

NLE
27 rue de Lisbonne
75008 Paris
nle-accounting.com

Spira, Twist & Associés
42 rue De Bassano
75008 Paris
spiratwist.com

Banks

Caisse d'Epargne (CE)
50 avenue Pierre
Mendès-France
75201 Paris
caisse-epargne.fr

Crédit Agricole (CA)
185 rue de Bercy
75012 Paris
credit-agricole.fr

Crédit Mutuel
88-90 rue Cardinet
75847 Paris
creditmutuel.fr

HSBC France
103 avenue des
Champs-Elysées
75419 Paris
hsbc.fr

ING Direct
Immeuble Lumière
40 avenue des Terroirs
de France 75564 Paris
ingwb.com

La Banque Postale
11 rue de Bourseul
75900 Paris
labanquepostale.fr

LCL
19 boulevard des Italiens
75002 Paris
lcl.com

Coffee Shops and Places with Wifi

Café Craft
24 rue des Vinaigriers
75010 Paris
cafe-craft.com

Coworkshop
29-32 rue des Vinaigriers
75010 Paris
coworkshop.fr

KB Caféshop South-Pigalle
53 avenue Trudaine
75009 Paris
kbcafeshop.com

L'Arobase Café
101 rue du Chevaleret
75013 Paris
arobasecafe.com

La Contrescarpe
57 rue Lacépède
75005 Paris

directory

La Fontaine de Belleville
31-33 rue Juliette Dodu
75010 Paris
lafontaine.cafesbelleville.com

Les P'tites Indécises
2 rue des 3 Bornes
75011 Paris

Strada Café
94 rue du Temple
75003 Paris
stradacafe.fr

Expat Groups and Meetups

Expats Paris
expats-paris.com

Expatriates in Paris
facebook.com/groups/expatri-
atesinparis

InterNations
internations.org/paris-expats

Meetup – Expats Paris
meetup.com/ExpatsParis

Flats and Rentals

Appartager
appartager.com

Find A Place In Paris
findaplaceinparis.com

Logic-Immo
logic-immo.com

PAP
pap.fr

Paris Attitude
parisattitude.com/
expats-apartments-rentals

Rent A Place In France
rentaplaceinfrance.com

Seloger
seloger.com

Important Government Offices

Business France
77 boulevard Saint-Jacques
75014 Paris
businessfrance.fr

Creative Paris
9 rue Delouvain
75019 Paris
creativefrance.fr

International Chamber of Commerce
Palais léna, 33-43 avenue du
Président Wilson
75116 Paris
iccwbo.org

Ministry of Economy and Finance
139 rue de Bercy
75572 Paris
economie.gouv.fr

Organisation for Economic Co-operation and Development
2 rue André Pascal
75775 Paris
oecd.org

Incubators in the City

Blue Factory
81 avenue de la République
75011 Paris
blue-factory.eu

Day One Entrepreneurs & Partners
13 rue de Marivaux
75002 Paris
dayonepartners.com

Nextstars
77 rue La Boétie
75008 Paris
nextstars.fr

Scientipole
Bureau 401
46 rue René Clair
75018 Paris
scientipole-idf.com

Sensecube
11 rue Biscornet
75012 Paris
paris.sensecube.cc

Startup42
14 rue Voltaire
94270 Le Kremlin-Bicêtre
startup42.org

Techstars Paris Partech Shaker
33 rue du Mail
75002 Paris
techstars.com

Usine IO
181 rue du Chevaleret
75013 Paris
usine.io

Insurance Companies

AXA
25 avenue Matignon
75008 Paris
axa.fr

Balance Health International
76 rue du Vertbois
75003 Paris
bilansanteinternational.com

Challenger V
16 rue Saint Charles
75015 Paris
challengerv.fr

Groupama
8 -10 rue d'Astorg
75008 Paris
groupama.fr

MSH International
18 rue de Courcelles
75384 Paris
msh-intl.com

RSA France
153 rue Saint Honoré
75001 Paris
fr.rsagroup.com

Investors

Alven Capital Partners
1 place André Malraux
75001 Paris
alvencapital.com

Daphni
87 rue Réaumur
75002 Paris
daphni.com

Elaia Partners
54 rue de Ponthieu
75008 Paris
elaia.com

Hardware Club
59 rue Beaubourg
75003 Paris
hardwareclub.co

Idinvest Partners
117 avenue des
Champs-Élysées
75008 Paris
idinvest.com

Isai
10 B Avenue de la
Grande-Armée
75017 Paris
isai.fr

Partech Ventures
18 avenue de Messine
75008 Paris
partechventures.com

TheFamily
25 rue du Petit-Musc
75004 Paris
thefamily.co
Ventech

47 avenue de l'Opéra
75002 Paris
ventechvc.com

Language Schools

**Alliance française
Paris Ile-de-France**
101 boulevard Raspail
75270 Paris
alliancefr.org

Ecole l'Etoile
38 boulevard Raspail
75007 Paris
ecole-letoile.com

Elfe
15 rue Montmartre
75001 Paris
elfe-paris.com

**l'Institut de Langue
Française**
6 rue Daubigny
75017 Paris
ilf-paris.fr

Lalangue Paris
110 rue Réaumur
75002 Paris
lalangueparis.com

Startup Events

Drinkentrepreneurs
drinkentrepreneurs.org

Events at theFamily
meetup.com/TheFamily-
MeetupsParis

Femmepreneurs
france.femmepreneurs.org

Mash Up
mash-up.fr
Paris New Tech
meetup.com/Paris-New-Tech

Start in Paris
startinparis.com

Startup Grind Paris
startupgrind.com/paris

Startup Weekend Paris
startupweekend.org

Techlunch Paris
meetup.com/Tech-Lunch

Startup Funding Events

FrenchPitch
meetup.com/French-Pitch

**Le 27 fait son pitch
by La Pépinière 27**
pepiniere27.fr

Pitch My Startup
pitchmystartup.fr

**Startup Pitch by
Digital Business Club**
digitalbusinessnews.com/
le-club

**TheNextWomen Pitch
Competition**
thenextwomen.com/
pitch-competition

glossary

A

Accelerator
An organization or program that offers advice and resources to help small businesses grow

Acqui-hire
Buying out a company based on the skills of its staff rather than its service or product

Angel Investment
Outside funding with shared ownership equity

ARR
Accounting (or average) rate of return: calculation generated from net income of the proposed capital investment

B

B2B
(business-to-business)
The exchange of services, information and/or products from a business to a business

B2C
(business-to-consumer)
The exchange of services, information and/or products from a business to a consumer

BOM
(Bill of Materials)
The list of the parts or components required to build a product

Bootstrap
Self-funded, without outside investment

Bridge Loan
A short-term loan taken out from between two weeks and three years pending arrangement of longer-term financing

Burn Rate
The amount of money a startup spends

Business Angel
An experienced entrepreneur or professional who provides starting or growth capital for promising startups

C

C-level
Chief position

Canvas Business Model
A template for developing new or documenting existing business models

Cap Table
An analysis of the founders' and investors' percentage of ownership, equity dilution and value of equity in each round of investment

CMO
Chief marketing officer

Cold-Calling
The solicitation of potential customers who were not anticipating such an interaction

Convertible Note/Loan
A type of short-term debt often used by seed investors to delay establishing a valuation for the startup until a later round of funding or milestone

Coworking
A shared working environment

CPA
Cost per action

CPC
Cost per click

Cybersecurity
The body of technologies, processes and practices designed to protect networks, computers, programs and data from attack, damage or unauthorized access

D

Dealflow
Term for investors to refer to the rate at which they receive business proposals

Deeptech
Companies founded on a scientific discovery or meaningful engineering innovation

Diluting
A reduction in the ownership percentage of a share of stock caused by the issuance of new shares

E

Elevator Pitch
A short summary used to quickly define a product or idea

Exit
A way to transition the ownership of a company to another company

F

Fintech
Financial technology

Flex Desk
Shared desks in a space where coworkers are free to move around and sit wherever they like

I

Incubator
Facility established to nurture young startup firms during their early months or years

IP (Intellectual Property)
Intangible property that is the result of creativity, such as patents, copyrights, etc

IPO
(Initial Public Offering)
The first time a company's stock is offered for sale to the public

K

KPI
(Key Performance Indicator)
a measurable value that demonstrates how effectively a company is achieving key business objectives

L

Later-Stage
More mature startups/companies

Lean
Refers to 'lean startup methodology'; the method proposed by Eric Ries in his book for developing businesses and startups through product development cycles.

M

M&A
(Mergers and Acquisitions)
A merger is a combination of two companies to form a new company, while an acquisition is the purchase of one company by another in which no new company is formed

MAU
Monthly active user

MVP
Minimum viable product

P

P2P
A network created when two or more PCs are connected and sharing resources without going through a separate server

Pitch Deck
A short version of a business plan presenting key figures

PR-Kit (Press Kit)
Package of pictures, logos and descriptions of your services

Pro-market
A market economy/a capitalistic economy

R

Runtime
The amount of time a startup has survived

S

SaaS
Software as a service

Scaleup
Company that has already validated its product in a market, and is economically sustainable

Seed Funding
First round, small, early-stage investment from family members, friends, banks or an investor

Seed Investor
An investor focusing on the seed round

Seed Round
The first round of funding

Series A/B/C/D
The name of funding rounds coming after the seed stage

Shares
The amount of the company that belongs to someone

Startup
Companies under three years old, in the growth stage and becoming profitable (if not already)

SVP
Senior Vice President

Solopreneurs
somebody developing their own personal brand; not a company to hire employees

T

Term Sheet/Letter of Intent
The document between an investor and a startup including the conditions for financing (commonly non-binding)

TCP/IP protocols
Transmission Control Protocol and Internet Protocol

U

UX
(User experience design)
The process of enhancing user satisfaction by improving the usability, accessibility and pleasure provided in the interaction between the user and the product.

Unicorn
A company worth over US$1 billion

USP
unique selling point

V

VC (Venture Capital)
Outside venture capital investment from a pool of investors in a venture capital firm in return for equity.

Vesting
Employee rights to employer-provided assets over time, which gives the employee an incentive to perform well and remain with the company

VR
Virtual Reality

213

STARTUP GUIDE LONDON   The Entrepreneur's Handbook
STARTUP GUIDE VIENNA   The Entrepreneur's Handbook
STARTUP GUIDE COPENHAGEN   The Entrepreneur's Handbook
STARTUP GUIDE OSLO   The Entrepreneur's Handbook
STARTUP GUIDE TRONDHEIM   The Entrepreneur's Handbook
STARTUP GUIDE LISBON   The Entrepreneur's Handbook

About the Guide

Based on the idea of a traditional guidebook to carry with you everywhere, the guides are made to inspire a generation to become more successful entrepreneurs through case-stories, advice and expert knowledge. Useful for when you start a project or business, the guide gives insight on where to go, who to talk to and what not to miss from the local people who know the city best.

How we make the guides:

To ensure an accurate and trustworthy guide every time, we team up with a local city partner, ideally an established organization with experience in the local startup scene, who conducts a general call out to the local community to nominate startups, coworking spaces, founders, incubators and established businesses through an online submission form. These submissions are narrowed down to the top fifty selected companies and individuals. The local advisory board then votes anonymously for the final selection to represent the range of industries and startup stories in the city. The local team, in close collaboration with our editorial and design team in Berlin, then organize and conduct the necessary interviews, photoshoots and research, using local journalists and photographers. All content is then reviewed, edited and approved by the Startup Guide team in Berlin and Copenhagen HQ, who are responsible for the final design, layout and print production.

Who makes the guides:

Sissel Hansen – Founder / CEO

Jenna van Uden – Editor

Josh Raisher – Deputy Editor

Tim Rhodes – Production Manager

Maurice Redmond – Art Director

Sanjini Redmond – Illustrator

João Mira – Marketing and Sales Manager

Eglė Duleckytė – Community & Expansion Manager

Daniela Carducci – Photo Editor

Ted Hermann – Proofreader

Alex Render – Design Assistant

Contact us at info@startupeverywhere.com

#startupeverywhere

Startup Everywhere is a creative content and self-publishing company that produces the **Startup Guide**. We develop, produce and distribute high quality content and tools to help you navigate in the local and global startup scene. Tailored to aspiring entrepreneurs, founders, freelancers, startups, investors and enthusiasts, it is a place to find inspiration, advice, specific local information and access to a growing network.

 Email info@startupeverywhere.com to get in touch with us.

Startup Guide Maps

The perfect navigational companion to the Startup Guide.
Startup Guide Maps is available on **iOS** and **Android**,
the app features all the coworking spaces, incubators,
accelerators and cafés with wifi in the cities that have
a guide.

The Startup Everywhere Community

Join the global community for entrepreneurs, founders,
startups, investors and enthusiasts. Find your local network,
get feedback, and access talent, know-how and much more.

The Startup Guide Store

Order a copy online and begin exploring the local startup
scenes of Berlin, Copenhagen, Aarhus, Stockholm, Oslo,
Lisbon, Trondheim, London and Vienna, with many more
to come. You click, we ship.

 startupeverywhere.com

Follow us: instagram.com/startupeverywhere

With thanks to our **media, event and content sponsors**

bluenove
opening innovation:

one**Ragtime**

Les Echos
START

VIVΛ
TECHNOLOGY
15-16-17 JUIN / PARIS 2017

Event Partner
/ VivaTechnology

VivaTechnology is the world's new rendezvous for game changers, bringing the most innovative startups together with global digital transformation leaders. The three-day event will take place from June 15th to 17th, 2017 at Porte de Versailles in Paris. This year we are proud to include among our main partners Google, Cisco, ManpowerGroup, LVMH and BNP Paribas.

During this three-day event, VivaTech turns Paris into a celebration of the best innovations, opening its doors to the general public on the final day. Co-organized by Publicis Groupe, a global leader in marketing, communication and digital transformation, and Groupe les Echos, the leading economic information media outlet in France, VivaTech empowers startups and big companies to meet and transform themselves. It aims to be a place to connect, exchange ideas, invest and collaborate. The idea is to gather the world's innovators, tech-lovers and pioneers of the future in the same place to foster innovation – 50,000 attendees (including 7,000 CEOs, 5,000 startups, 20 unicorns and 1,000 investors) sharing a belief in the power of innovation with the goal of preparing business and society for the future.

Seventy percent of the speakers lined up for the main stage will be international, including David Kenny, GM of IBM Watson; Peter Fenton, general partner of Benchmark; Ambarish Mitra, cofounder and CEO of Blippar; Daniel Zhang, CEO of Alibaba; and many more. Thanks to the presence of internationally known media outlets including Bloomberg Media, CNN, TechCrunch, The Wall Street Journal and TF1, we will have wide coverage of the event.

The first iteration in 2016 proved that France has a viable startup ecosystem with an international presence. The 2017 event will bring back our signature three-day Labs, where startups will cowork with leading businesses on their challenges to find solutions that will go to market. Twenty Labs, each focused on a sector, are being sponsored by leaders like Cisco, LVMH and AccorHotels. Each will hand-pick the brightest startups in their category to help them solve today's most pressing digital transformation problems listed on our Challenges open innovation platform. Startups can win a Lab place by applying to solve one of these challenges. It's a classic win-win: big companies gain fresh insight into their business' challenges, and startups get access to companies, VCs and programs looking for new talent. It's a once-in-a-lifetime opportunity to collaborate and champion growth.

Visit **challenges.vivatechnology.com** for more info.

Paris

Media Partner
/ Les Echos START

Les Echos START is a French online and print media outlet created in late 2015 dedicated to helping young adults start their professional lives. It delivers current news, useful tips and videos on employment and jobs opportunities, expat life and startups. As more and more young adults decide to build their own companies or join the startup ecosystem, Les Echos START connects its readers to the community's key actors through exclusive news and reports on entrepreneurs, incubators, accelerators, VCs and influencers. It also gives voices to young entrepreneurs to tell their stories and share their experiences on its website through authentic testimonies to show the diversity of paths available and inspire wannabe founders.

Les Echos START serves as a real mentor and coach for young adults in the Paris ecosystem who want to build their own companies or identities. It helps them to identify innovation and business trends, the drivers that improve their business development strategies, and teaches them how to pitch their projects and raise funding. It give them many opportunities to discover and follow the "game changers" in various sectors, including social business, fintech, tech and media. Through interviews and live videos, Les Echos START chats every week with major actors within the ecosystem, including Roxane Varza of Station F, the biggest incubator in the world, opening summer 2017 in Paris; Alexandre Malsh, cofounder of Meltygroup; Loic Le Meur, who recently launched Leade.rs in Paris; and many others. It regularly make Facebook Live videos inside French startups so that its audience gets a behind-the-scenes glimpse into how it is to work in these innovative and dynamic environments. And the startups get a chance to discuss their products, their experiences as startupers and their hiring targets with entrepreneurs. It also covers major tech events such as CES, Slush, South by Southwest and, in June 2017, VivaTech.

WHERE NEXT?